Elements of hope

James Carroll

Published by Pastoral Educational Services
Special Projects Division of
Paulist Press
400 Sette Drive, Paramus, New Jersey 07652

President: Rev. Kevin A. Lynch, C.S.P.
Vice President and Project Director:
Rev. Thomas E. Comber, C.S.P.

Editor and Photographic Selection: Joseph W. Nash
Design: Ron Cutro Associates, Tenafly, N. J.

Picture Credits:
Ray Gora—Pages: Cover, end sheets, 26, 27, 35, 54,
60, 63, 70, 82, 105, 106
George Hoffmann—Pages: 7, 13, 36, 41, 44, 64,
84, 85, 102, 103, 107
Joseph A. Nash—Pages: 22, 23, 74
Tony Roberts—Pages: 9, 10
Ed Lettau—Pages: 50, 53, 99
Berne Greene—Pages: 20, 38, 49, 80, 87, 92, 94
Pete Lang—Pages: 4, 5, 17, 30, 56, 58, 72, 89, 109
Thomas J. Connellan—Pages: 8, 59
Joseph W. Nash—Pages: 46, 47, 65
George Egley—Pages: 18, 25, 29, 42, 95, 100, 110

(Black Star):
Robert Goodman—Pages: 66, 67, 76

NASA Photo—Page: 34

Library of Congress
Catalog Card Number: 76-173699   PS 3553.A764E4

Color Separations by:
Color Control Corp., Little Ferry, N. J.

Printed and bound in the
United States of America by:
R. R. Donnelley & Sons Co., Chicago, Ill.
G.T.O. Lithographers, Inc., Little Ferry, N. J.

Contents

Section 1
Elements of Hope

One: Beginnings

We must make the best of bad beginnings.
In that way we follow God of the Genesis poem,
whose beginning was worse than ours,
even worse than ours.
Like a big bird he hovered, ah bright wings!,
over chaos, over emptiness, over night
darker even than this night of our souls.
We have destroyed not only forests
but the bodies of Asian children
and the beauty of our names.
Like a big bird he hovered, breathing
out of emptiness, air; shaping
out of chaos, earth; loving
out of darkness, fire; stirring
out of nothing, water; pulling form,

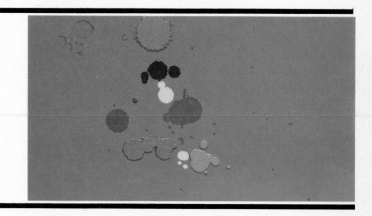

Beginnings

pulling color, pulling fragrance,
pulling even laughter from the world-wide pit
of that bad beginning.
Here we are
at bad beginnings again.
A world-wide pit of chaos
reaching to our souls;
cities out of air and we cannot breathe,
concrete deserts out of earth
and we cannot grow,
passions of flesh out of fire
and we cannot love,
thirsty rivers out of water
and we cannot drink, or drink
nothing but draughts of fear and memory.
There were better beginnings than this
when we were virgin with our dreams.
We have destroyed not only forests

but the bodies of Asian children
and the beauty of our names.
We were virgin with our dreams.
Earth was where the seeds went, joyfully.
Fire was light and warmth to gather 'round.
Water washed us of our guilt, quickened us.
Air refreshed our hearts on mornings of glory.
Remember with me another childhood
when virgins were not victims of commerce gods,
when earth was not chained to machines of no-love,
when air was not poison,
when fire was not a rain of death nor napalm,
when water was our swimming pond with live fish.
Remember with me another childhood, another May
when we were too alive to talk of life,
too ready for the future to talk of hope.
Those were days when meaning was not packaged
and we could laugh at preachers in their grimness.

We have destroyed not only forests
but the bodies of Asian children
and the beauty of our names.
But we must make the best of bad beginnings.
This is not the end
but our only place to start from.
We spring yet with a yearning to live
that will end our killing if we let it.
We still wake with a vision of earth
that denies our doubting, forbids the remorse
that does not lead to new work, old play
in the names of the men and women
we would, with some adventure, be still.
Guilt is not allowed in morning.
Only penance, briskly felt and turned to service.
Can you believe with me still,
though faith is gone,
in the kingdom we forgot?

The kingdom called once for all out of chaos.
If we live close to chaos now
yet are we close to the kingdom,
close as any heart, however hesitant its pulse.
Can you love with me yet
this universe, its energies, its secrets,
its earth, still good,
its air, still unmasked at least,
its fire, sign of night's hope,
its water, quenching, even inexpensive?
Dare we hope to love each other yet?
And our forests?
And Asian children?
And our names?
Yes, ah bright wings, yes!
For listen to the faint fluttering;
look to the window, wipe its haze and see
an old big bird beating against our pain,
all shades of light and color,
calling yet a kingdom out of chaos,
good soil out of desert,
water out of thirst,
air out of all suffocation,
fire out of apathy,
life out of even our death-making,
laughter out of even our grim preaching.

Warm wings that have made the best
of worse beginnings than even this,
spread like young trees under which
we can be young and easy with each other
as once we were in another May.
Listen. See. Breathe quietly.
It is the hovering bird that flies eternally
from the center of the sun, ah bright wings,
from the gentle edge of God's care.

Two: April just in time

It is April again and just in time.
A difficult winter it was for us,
for the earth, for the air, for the poor water.
Difficult for me surely, and you, I think.
Difficult for all but the fire
which was not frozen out but only banished
to that warmer climate; lucky fire
spent the winter thriving in the jungle.
Does anything thrive there but fire?
The tree outside my second-floor window
has had enough of the cold, enough of
that grey sickness of air and sky
the calendar calls February.
I have had enough of that grey sickness
of deep down spirit

which has no name yet
but which you and I have been less secret with lately.
This tree outside my hazy window
through which I saw hovering birds before
needs sun, warmth
and the green tickle of new buds.
And I *outside your hazy window?*
need words of hope.
It is that simple.
Do you need words of hope too?
Ah, then brother put it there!
What a winter, eh? Hell, wasn't it?
What with that war and all the depressing news,
the taxes and the kids rioting even in
high school and not being altogether wrong.
My best friend's daughter is using heroin.
The whole world needs professional help, you know?
And words of hope.
Here I am sitting down to write again.
For you, maybe, since we are closer
I suspect
than either of us know.
But for me surely, for sitting down to write
is my best way of making sense,
of making hope.
Write what? Not theology, for sure.
Not music either. Something in between,
between God-talk and love songs.
These are one man's notes
on the humming of his soul.
You have to smile a little, don't you?
I mean, why do I hem and haw?
Because I dance around the important thing,
get off it quick if it begins to show—
how much I need not only words of hope
but your love. I am embarrassed again.
These words come not only of my need
but of the fullness of life's gift.
I am passionate about this world.
I love its evenings and rain, its forests,

its careful mothers, its sweet smells,
the banks of its rivers, its leaves,
its tennis balls, its bus drivers.
I live for this world,
the bottoms of its oceans, its candles,
its lifeguards, its mountain climbers,

its baby buggies, its old men.
I love the spirit at its center,
its white fires, its women,
its rocks, its bells, its moon.
I love the tree outside my window,
its buds, its courage, its stubborness.
I love the earth.
I love the air.

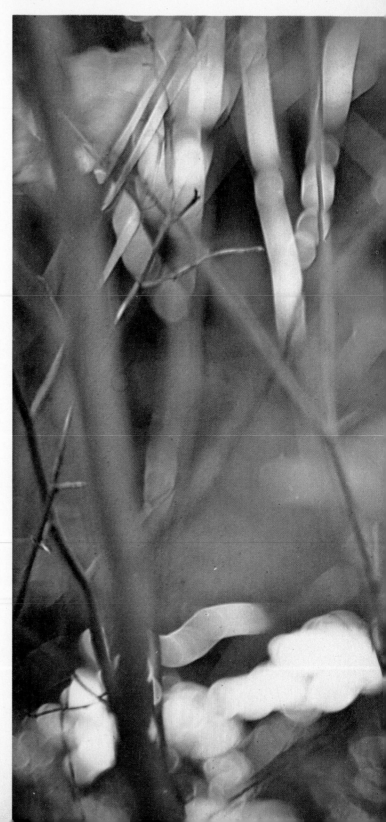

I love the fire.
I love the water.
They are the metaphors of my soul.
I celebrate them.
I ask forgiveness of them.
I hum their music and know their melody
by heart, by blood, by flesh.
Like laughter, they refuse my attempts

to render them abstract and therefore empty.
It is April, finally,
and here I am humming to you
of earth, fire, water, air;
elements of life and of our brotherhood
and words of hope enough for now.

Three: Not without promise

My editor keeps saying
"Jim, the thing to remember is 'why is this book
imperative at this particular point in time?'"
I say to myself
"What could possibly be 'imperative' about one
minor priest humming to himself on an April
afternoon?"
You have to smile a little, don't you?
We both know nothing is imperative anymore.
Except ending the war and feeding people.
Certainly not another book.
This book is definitely not imperative.
Neither am I. Nor are you.
This book is probably not even important.
Ah, but I am. So are you.
Important, yes. We are all we have.
I'll tell you what else is important;
water drawn painfully
out of my eyes;
fire drawn gingerly
out of my heart;
air drawn wistfully
from my breathings in and out;
earth scooped up carefully
out of the dirt.
Dirt becomes earth when we love it.
Next time I will say to my editor,
"Tom, baby, it is important at this particular time
because we should not be without words
in a season of effort.
We should not be without a promise
in the April of planting.
We should not be without thanks
in the summer of harvest."
He will understand what we mean
because, in addition to being an editor,
he is a man.

One: Everyday the wedding night

Every day the wedding night.
We assist continually at the marriages
of earth, air, fire and water.
But we do not notice.
We are bored, where once men
were knocked to their knees.
We smile at our first fathers
who thought God pulled a special stick,
opening the heavens to make it rain.
They were so simple, silly even, eh?
Yet they would smile at us
for not knowing the secret of the heavy rain;
that there are lovers hidden in the soil
waiting to be ravished; there are lovers

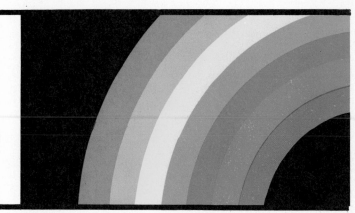

2 The loving eyes of hope

in the falling streams, anxious, lustful.
They fell, our first fathers,
to their knees at the crack of thunder,
half, yes, out of superstitious fear,
but half as well out of delight at love.
The worst storms were an ecstacy for everyone.
We cover our heads with newspaper
and run away, prudishly, children
who do not yet know of their parents' pleasure.
We miss the marriage bed of rain and soil
because we think men were made for moderation.
Our silly first fathers knew, with thunderbolts,
that men were made for ecstacy.
It is true, what we said as children
on the way to church;
"Those pagans had more fun than us!"
Why should we fear getting wet

if air is not afraid of mating with fire
and leaving love's lightning wreckage
all over the August sky?
Let us be uncensored long enough to know
that rain makes more than mud with earth;
it makes love.
Can we dance at that?
Can we be unneat enough to kiss the soil?
Soil, the first bride?
No thunder's shock, no, nor no caressing wind
can compare with the passion
of the union of ourselves with this universe
when we are there and joining in
the marriage of the elements.
Then our first and last loneliness is lifted.
No vision of angels, no, nor no flight of holiness
can compare with the awful horror and joy
that seizes us when, beneath ordinariness,
under everyday, we see the wedding night
of air and fire and water and earth.
The life begun is ours.
And what is finally born
is the world again
and more;
it is the only God we know.

Two: The thing is not to ask God too many questions

The thing is not to ask God too many questions
because He is dumb.
He does not answer.
He waits till things are simpler,
next year perhaps. There will be an answer.
Who was that answer
holding your hand last night?
The thing is not to think
of God as a nice fellow
because, take it from me, He is tough.
If you let him
he will scorch your hair with fire,
he will drown you nearly naked with his water,
the air of his breath can be just awful
and he will surely bury you with earth.
Hope is a matter of lowered expectations.
It is when the great marble statue topples
of the comforting God
who tucks you in his safest pocket,

of the magic mystery
who always makes things better—
when it topples, though you flee,
on your head,
it is then that the real God
of Job's old fight stands up, glaring.
What else is there to say from
the pile of ruined expectations but
"Hope is not what I thought it was."
Or, "Even though you slay me
and He will
I will trust you."
Which is another way of saying
"My God, My God
You must be kidding!"
Hope like that is hard,
especially for Narcissists like us.
The thing is not to take God too seriously,
because, by our standards,
God is slightly crazy.
Who was that mental health
you were with the other day?
Here is hope; by His standards,
we are slightly crazy too.
And that is what you and I
and God have in common;
common craziness.
Theologians call it grace.

Three: How to survive both politics & poetry

You have a lot of nerve, don't you?
Sitting there, reading, humming to yourself,
laughing at theologians
while half the world starves.
Why aren't you out baking bread
or getting arrested or something?
How can you talk about grace
without feeling guilty?
The faint refrain still haunts us;
we have destroyed not only forests
but the bodies of Asian children
and the beauty of our names.
What is grace, what even is hope
and what are these thin words
while the dragon
is wrecking still the world?

Especially the world that is not
white and wealthy.
How can we worry about words
when the dragon wrecks the world
and claims its blood on our behalf?
What do we mourn most?
Our lovely names or the lives of
all those children or California trees?
Can we hope at least that our humming
together in this way is more out
of life than death?
Can we ask forgiveness in this way
of each other, of our victims,
of the Spirit we have forgotten?
And could it even be
that the dragon slays
out of burdens of guilt we do not know
and, in its heart, helpless,
looks to us for help, forgiveness?
If we worry about words let them be
only the words of life which raped forests,
slain children, ruined names
carry in their souls, still yearning
to be spoken with care.
We may not have innocence enough
to accuse an entire age of narrowness
but we can stand with our weak voices
saying, "We choose to end the slaying.
We choose to savor life, beauty, childishness
not beyond, but in our streets."
There is craziness
amazing craziness enough in us
if not to be innocent forever
at least to laugh once more
before bed tonight.
Shall we dare to rid ourselves
of guilt for sorrow?
Shall we forget our well-adjustment
long enough to say next time they ask
"How are you?",
"Even though you slay me
not bad at all"?
And when next we hesitate
before words of grace, beauty,
solitude, family love, playfulness,
can we dare to tell the dragon

who would distract us
"We <u>are</u> baking bread—bread of our
hunger that you might eat
instead of slay."
The inwardness we seek
is of the spirit-kind that plunges
to the depths, not of lonely selves,
but of this wrecked world
in which creation is still given.
The politics we seek is not
an art of old possibilities
but an art of finding new ones.
The poetry we seek
is not the work of hermits
but of nations who need with us
to learn the earth and its fullness.
The grace we seek
is what happens when all the flowers
in the garden of fire are just right.
They are so right that, until now,
we have not noticed.
We learned early from NBC
that only ungracefulness is interesting.
Only what is sane
and sanitary is safe.
You do have a lot of nerve,
and you need it to notice life.
Noticing-life is another word for hope.

Because the fired stars move
so well together, with such high grace,
we do not see them.
Because the red water of our veins
strives so faithfully for our fingers
we do not feel it.
We never miss what does not fit.
We are visionaries of violence,
and so servants of it.
We are experts at what goes wrong,
and so disheartened.
The dragon we fear in guilt
is the child of our boredom.
We are blind to the harmonies
of minor life
and so ruthless with all other.
If, for example, sunrise were an accident,
a one-time eccentricity,
dawn would find us
gathered on the beach,
murmuring, cameras ready, microphoned.
But the sun is no accident,
neither is blood, nor topsoil,
nor playground basketball, nor spring,
nor low laughter, nor rain.
It is all grace dancing.
We were given nerve to notice.
We were given legs to dance along.

One: The experience of alienation

One potato, two potato,
In the last fifty years
three potato, four
we normal, good meaning men
five potato, six potato
have slaughtered by our own hands
seven potato
one hundred millions of ourselves!
Or! We all lose.
If we could feel that truth,
remove it from this page,
make it more heart than history,
we would be changed enough to dull
the edge of annihilation that waits
to destroy us all.

3 Toward elemental awareness

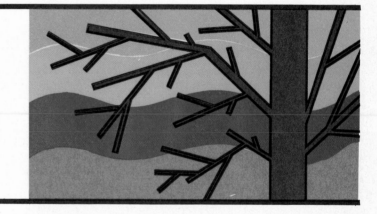

Is it any wonder we are alone,
untrusting, as afraid to live as to die?
Is it any wonder our new name
for violence is love?
How many times have I killed you
out of fear you would eat my bread
which then went stale
since I could not eat
it all alone?
If you are a man
chances are I compete with you,
may destroy you in my need to win.
If you are a woman
chances are I murder you,
with fantasies, part mother, part maid,
lover enough to ease my stress.
If you are a child
chances are I resent you already.

If you are old and tired
I have forgotten you, likely,
in your attic room alone.
The chances are good, all of them,
because I am as normal as you are.
Don't you know that it's a fool
who plays it cool, Lennon says,
when his soul is freezing?
We have a great future, they say.
But then we have always had.
You and I know how far the future is
when you go there on your knees.
It began, the story says,
by loving too little a single tree.
When it comes to Tao or Logos
or creation more captive than given
the instinct has been more to
exploit *another word for hit on the head*
than cooperate *another word for kiss.*
We know how to waste the earth,
ruin its soil, ravage its forests,
poison its air, pour filth into its rivers.
Loveless nature gave us floods,
tundra, tombs, deserts.
Loveless men gave nature famine,
pollution, war and thirst,
mass producing death,
technologizing scarcity of love.
We know how to waste everything.
What we do not know
is the name of one of those
one hundred millions dead.
Could we but take him in our arms
and say, "You are mine, you are me."
Could we stop saying then
"I regret, but what could I do?
Your death is modern war,
is economy at work, is power balancing."
Who are we to embrace our victims?
Who are we to get up from our knees?
And be awakened to the world?
Who are we to change death into life?
Who are we to talk at all of love?
Who are we to wait for God?
Yet, who are we to say it is hopeless?
If there was a time, and it is not past,

18

when we could slap each other's fist
singing *"one potato, two potato,"*
learning even then about earth's apples,
"three potato four"
without masquerades of love
"five potato, six potato"
though the dreadful had already happened
"seven potato"
and we knew it.
"Or!", who are we to lose?

Two: The genesis garden

The Pit, of all places,
is least rare.
All pits are shallow
except for the deep ones
and they are deeper than cruelty.
When you have laid your cheek
against the dirt
for less than a moment
which is a lifetime,
wailed against the wall
which is low, but too high;
when you have knelled down death
to kiss the mouth of dust,
hoping to wring out
one last tongue of rain,
darkness holds you hard.
No one hears the thirsty bell
of burial, least of all you.
The pit man is rare as water,
the one true stranger,
only one unstrange.
All pits assemble at his tongue.
He gardens them,
unearthly flood of care,
nursing bones side by side,
raking down walls with the soft
first strokes of ringing sighs.
O you who, for the desert
of that time
could neither drink nor cry,
break a boulder tear of joy
to join the pit man's
sprinkle of delight.
Our pitted yard

is the garden again
and he, gardener-like,
unrecognized at first,
walks in the cool
not of evening
but of dawn.

Three: A certain sacramental presence

Wherever men abandon hope
despair waits to be overcome.
The earth, the wind,
the fire, the rain
have great expectations of us
for they remember what we forget;
you and I and aldermen and artists
and chemists and soldiers
and city planners
and students and presidents
are, all of us, human beings!
We can imagine the world!
We can remove the leaves
from our naked skin.
When we stand in and carry
within ourselves the same presence
alienation fades before union.
Even business with its receipts
waits to withdraw to the margins
of importance, waits for us to recover
the splendor of mystery, profitless,
serving no end but intimacy.
Silence waits, not to be avoided,
but to be improved upon
by the awkward speech of true men.
Swords wait to be swallowed
as fire waits to be eaten with relish.
The ambiguous world cannot forget

its old secret, that more lives
in its elements and their mingling
than eyes of flesh can see.
April is naked to eyes of rain,
August to eyes of fire.
Eyes of earth and wind
see sacraments everywhere.
It is the business of creation
to make God concrete without apology.
We need not return to Eden
or forget the cities we have made
or murder our machines
to speak of God without blushing.
The wind is not embarrassed
both to turn turbines
and whisper of presences beyond.
Water can wash engines
and lay quite still, beguiled
by what it knows of peace.
It is neither an old nor newer
world we need,
but a way of seeing what clings
to the underside of everything,
man made or found.
The question clings as well,
the only one in the end
as in the beginning:
how to meet and learn to love
the one whose terrible splendor
goes far beyond our poor
but only word, God?
The earth, the wind,
the fire, the rain,
unless they lie and our blindness is true,
bid us wait here,
bid us wait and watch with care.

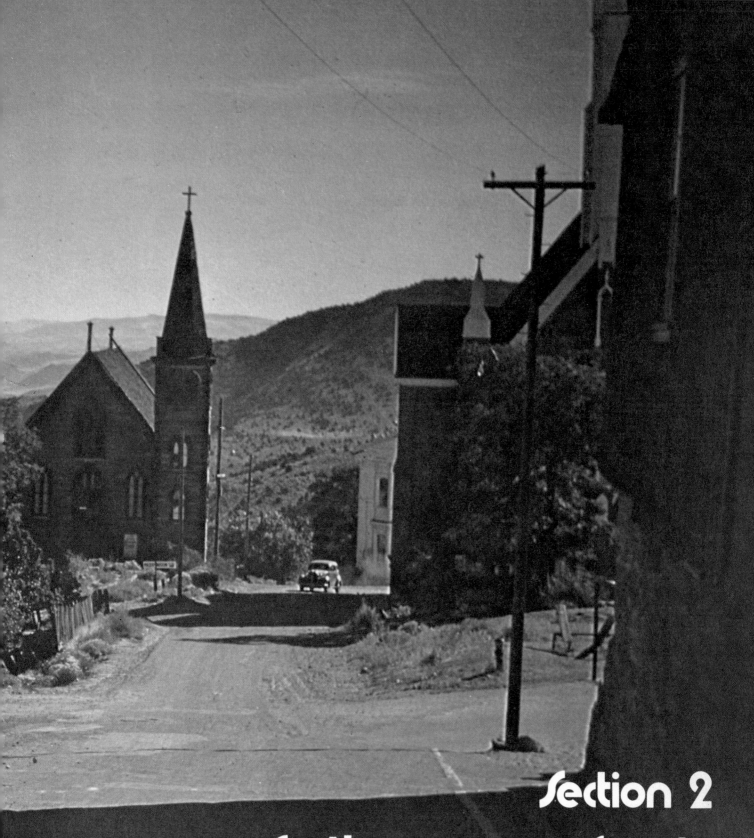

Section 2
Earth-recovery of roots

One: More mileage than mother

An old Wintu Indian said
before they killed him
"Wherever white man has touched
the earth it is sore."
The old Indian would be glad to know
the earth is sore no more,
for we have banished it from our world.
Earth is not allowed where we live
except in safe patches,
captured in yards,
caged with fences, looked at.
Do not walk, we say.
Do not feed the grass with your flesh.
When was the last time you
bared your feet to the soil?

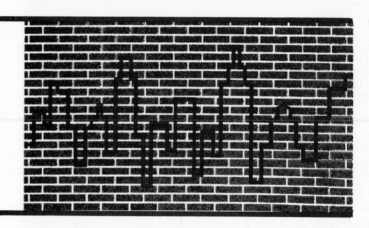

4 Earthlessness

The earth is not sore
because we never touch it anymore.
Where once we ruined our knees
and gloved our fingers with mud,
which was the earth's way of loving us,
our sons roll on astroturf.
The best minds of industry
struggle to keep us off the dirt
as if it would poison us.
And we pay them.
What do we do to children
when earth stains are punished,
when they are locked into
playgrounds, strange name, of tar,
painted lines, plumbing for trees?
Do you remember the paths
you wore across the field, going home?
Was the earth worse for your feet?

Is it better for asphalt?
We have learned to defeat
our own best yearnings;
when cities were crowded
we yearned for open fields
and cool worm-ridden dirt
between our toes.
So we bought a car, like everyone,
and drove to where they said
the fields of harvest would be.
We bought our house and our future
and parked our car, like everyone
where the field of harvest
should have been.
We tried to return to earth,
but our car got stuck.
So we settled for returning to tar.
What did we lose?
Going barefoot from April to August
is not so much, after all.
There are no bad bounces on astroturf.
Artificial earth is better.
And now that the highways are,
at a million a mile, finished,
it's so easy to go someplace,
though harder to have
someplace to go.
We are joined to our families,
our friends *the crowds we flee*
and to our mother earth
by the best roadways in the world.
We whizz by each other now,
and by hills, hidden valleys,
general stores, farms, stagnant ponds,
oak trees from the colonies,
harvests, dug up fields, caves,
small rivers with their mermaids.
And what do we see?
Green exit signs, the speedometer,
white stripes, endless ribbons
of grey guardrails,
the speedometer,
billboards with beer,
restaurants with orange roofs,
gas stations that have
bathrooms cleaner than home,

the speedometer,
Volkswagons every other car,
green exit signs, white stripes
and the speedometer.
When you get there finally
do you brag too about your
average speed and mileage?
Who needs mother earth
when you have three good lanes?
The old Wintu Indian
from his place below pavement
smiles likely, don't you think?
He and the poor earth
he loved enough to worry about
have their revenge, perhaps.
It is what happens when men
think themselves too good
for getting dirty feet or moving slowly.
It is what happens when men
seek to trade their earth
for a home of angels:
they think themselves successful

and they call it Los Angeles.

Two: Roots of uprootedness

From the mirror earth
holds up to us we turn;
the likeness it works upon shivers us.
Those eyes—we cannot look at them,
for we begin to lay claim
on their melancholy as our own.
The earth on which we seek a home
expresses the inner earth
of our souls to ourselves.
Shall we scavenge, though Luke warned us,
among the dead for the living?
In the center of the mirror
the earth holds is a great uprooted tree,
roots helpless in the air,
casualty of concrete, of ruthless progress.
Those dangling roots, we cannot look at them,
for we begin to lay claim
on their blood as our own.
We are bleeding at the roots,

at the lifelines of the past
which are fingers to the future.
Ah, but you say, we are men,
not trees; alive, not dead.
Look again at the reflecting earth,
the landscape of tossed branches.
Those twisted creatures crossing it,
each with his load, lost,
search for soil in which to plant
their remaining seeds.
They are you and me.
The land forgives.
It waits for us.
The mirror the earth holds
meets us with a question for trees and men;
how do we plant ourselves again?
Trees will take care of themselves.
They always have.
For us, we must not dream
of returning to incense or horses,
or farming even.
We do live now, after all.
The roots of our nourishing,
of human kind, are fine, subtle.
We need to learn to love life
and all of its signs, its things even,
as ends and not as means.
That lack is what ruins
earth and us.
We are not trees, but men;
you were right
our roots have names;
work, law, leisure, mind, learning,
erotic love, family, religion,
friendship, solitude, freedom.
These are fingers hung in air,
deprived of soil where
past grows into futures worth having.
I would not ask "who am I?"
if I knew; I would not talk
of roots if they were planted.
Learning is no utility's hoard
of packages of meaning,
but what happens when you grow.
Work is not the drudgery of wages
but how we build the world.

Law is not the leveling of differences
but how we celebrate them.
Leisure is not recovering from effort
for the next one's sake,
but contemplation for its own.
Mind is not merely means
to possession and power
but a way to stand under the world.
Erotic love is no escape from fear
but man and woman fearful for each other.
Family is not an isolated fortress
but the common gift to every life.
Religion is not a trick played on God
but a language for speaking mystery.
Friendship is not a device for promotion
but the company of failures.
Solitude is not an interlude of presence
but the shadow of eternity.
Freedom is not self-grandeur
but a chance for reckless service.
Earth is not the road to other worlds
but the simple start of heaven.
We can throw wide our seeds again
and wash them down earth's throat
with the sharp taste of blood
our old roots still shed.
There are roots beyond our rootlessness
that even now reach through the sand
to soil, bedrock, and another world
that is born here.
We are not trees, but men.
You were right.
The smashed faces of our past heal
though we ignore them.
I have walked the shore for hours
where earth weeps for us into oceans,
but the tides, with spirit we forget,
kept elbowing me to the land again,
to earth where seeds not only die
but start over endlessly.
The oneness of all elements
in the universe, which includes us,
has a root we know not of,
one common source of being
awake all night in earth's cellar,
refusing the final fall of any tree,

forcing it into new soil of life,
forcing us, earth, you and me
to be roots to each other.

Three: Memories of mudpies (or, how I learned to love the earth)

It was mud that first
enchanted me.
After summer's rain I would
sneak out the back way,
knowing enough already not to wear
my Sunday shirt.
Water waited in small pools
on the path by the fence,
a carpet before me of mud,
no grass to come between the dirt and me.
How gloriously the earth got wet.
Thwack! And a hunk of muck
was mine, caught in my small hands.
You start by slapping it, rolling
the water out, kneading the death out.
Thwack! Smack it flat, press it,
let it ooze between your fingers once.
Thwack! Slap it again.
My hands lost themselves in brown gloves,
fast and shaping without thought.
Roll, caress, ball it up,

tongue watching from the corner
of my careful mouth.
Then thwack again! Gentler, though,
the final flattening, fragile shaping
into a nickel pie of mud.
Set it over there to dry. Ah!
Another fist, then. Another hunk.
Thwack again, another pie.
It was my first art,
my first gift of form,
though I didn't think of it
as anything but mud.
It was what made rain make sense,
my own harvesting
of the seeds of perfection
hidden in the dirt.
My first partnership with earth.
When they told me on Sundays
about Creation Morning
when God scooped up slime
to make that fellow Adam,
I knew already what He was up to.
I knew the pure delight
of giving what you make away.
I knew what that first
Thwack! was like.
The earth had taught me.

One: Priest at a friend's graveside

In the morning trek of burial
we climb the hill
to the graveside of our friend.
The light rain trickles
with the moisture of our noses.
*Does it always rain
on funeral days?*
We do not speak, save my
priest-muttering,
"Remember, man, you are earth
and unto earth
you shall return."
I see the gravediggers
hovering in covered shade
of the cemetery oak,

5 I am earth

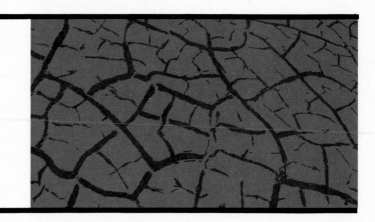

waiting to finish up.
One leans on his shovel.
They are my partners,
dealing, as priests and diggers do,
in decay, buried hearts.
I see them and think
we feed on lost lives,
we share a diet of death.
They complain against life
with their shovels, with their backs,
I with musty words
some saint or whoring monk
or both bequeathed the church.
Since, at this moment,
no words matter, you may
as well speak them with fervor;
"O God, we commend to your
all merciful care your servant . . ."

We stand here, heads bowed,
hands awkward, not listening,
not talking, yet each saying
in his own way,
"You took the one I loved,
don't take me."
Through my droning prayers,
which God may hear,
though no one else does,
voices of the grave begin to speak;
"Remember, priest, you are earth."
I look down into the pit
that waits for my dead friend.
"Unto earth you shall return."
And I know it is not him
I fear for, or worry over.
It is myself and my company
of graveside mourners.
I think of him, dead man
with a living name, completed
pilgrim, planted seed.
He is earth.
Which is the grave's way
of saying in his death
he is life. He knows.
But we, in our muttering,
do not as yet know.
So, priest, burier of hearts,
I repeat, speaking to the living,
"Remember, you are earth.
And unto earth you shall return."
I smile, hoping not to violate
our agreed upon grimness,
thinking everyday is earth day
when you're dead.
But when you live, as we do,
words mean least when
you need them most.
All of us must stand
in light rain, not listening
to the droning saint, the whoring monk,
the grim priest, awkward
with our hands, dying when
we want to live.
I think of my lost friend
whom I miss already.

The heaving thighs of his life,
mother, father both,
have given birth to him again,
though we call him death.
If we were born twice,
e.e. said, most of us
would call it dying.
Our words fail us,
for the earth speaks not,
though voices of the grave
break through my muttering.
"Remember, you are earth."
I touch the soil with my loss,
gently take it to cover him,
returning my friend to earth,
dipping belief in the dew
of all the bleak dawns
our dead loves leave with us
as we too wait.

Two: Astronaut's log (deletion)

The moon, finally, was no surprise.
As we always thought, dead, dusty.
Not much to it, really.
You prepared us well for that.
But not so well for other things.
The silence, for example.
You never said it would be so still,
so unearthly still, quiet.
Or did you know?
Even as the data grew
and the little clicks continued,
silence settled over us.
And we were not prepared for that.
Did you know there is nothing
to look at from up here
but the old earth itself?
Nor were we prepared for that.
The moon was no surprise,
but the earth was.
We find it awkward,
embarrassing almost, to look
from our black window on
that blue green ball where
you are, where we were once,
where we hope to be again.

We were not prepared
to look from silence on our own
earth, our own earth there.
We did not know the earth
till now. Isn't that strange?
We had to leave the place
to see it at all.
Maybe it's the black nothing
in which the earth floats, hangs
that grabs you most.
We never knew how close
to nothing our own place is.
We feel odd feelings.
How do we get data here?
Earth hangs in nothing;
how do you program that?
Earth looks very small,
helpless almost from here.
We feel funny looking at it,
at you, as if we caught
you in a mistake, a blunder.
Strange, but we are protected
against mistakes out here,
but earth is not.
You are more vulnerable than we are.
We are embarrassed for you.
But you are protected from silence
and from the black nothing
and from the odd feelings.
You are protected from
earth's vulnerability,
from embarrassment.
You are smaller than we are.
We worry for you, earth.
You are very close to nothing.
You must be more careful with yourself.
As careful as you are with us.
We are silent for you.
You did not prepare us for this;
to look back on you with love.

Three: Earth's ecstacy; fragments from her diary

The man with aimless grinning
who plows my womb
and furrows my belly for his seed
awaits the year's turning

for my small return on his labor.
He thinks I am his.
He thinks his limpid harvest
of corn and grain are my best fruit.
He measures my gestation
by his arbitrary calendar.
I smile at my lover, Sun,
whose lust and thrust have arched
me since God told his sorrow
to the universe
and we were mated.
Oh, Sun, sucking at my breast,
what are we to say of this seedling, man?
You and I forget passions
he has never known.
He is harsh, unmannerly in his youth.
He thinks himself aged,
latecomer to my fat plain,
novice to my gaunt wilderness.
What does he know?
He thinks his world changes,
and threatens us with his uproar,
his rage at insecurity, at turmoil.
What, next to me,
knows he of change?
He is lean of sight.
I know ecstacies he leaves untouched.
My horizons catch the swerve
of the hawk's wing still
and have done so since my
mountain taught the first hawk flight.
He does not see.
My swift grass in ancient habits
learned from winter ages
covers even now unsightly wounds
he opens on me, as if I
were an untouched maiden.
When I throw up spring meadows
with the hush of summer
and heal the graves he invents
he looks at me for hay.
My rich memories of crumbled
worlds he never knew,
though I hide them from his eye,
are not safe from his machine.
What remains of the crush

on my back between fire and ice
and shifting continents
he sees as gold and rapes me
and his own rare heritage.
He will take my courage
for his boxes; he calls it soil.
He will take my brittle hope
for his vase; he calls it flower.
When the first warbler sings to me
when the snow lays in my arms,
when I couple with the sky's blue axle
and the moon circles me with messages,
when cattle scratch my itches
and fumbling lambs scribble thanks
in the desolate pasture I offer
why are his screams in the dark
still shrill and meaningless?
Can he not see?
I favor the man, but he does not know.
Lately he is like a shadow to me;
he loses what glimmer of flesh
we shared in earlier times,
long, long ago to him,
just yesterday to me.
I wonder, will my crimson heather
and solitary brooks where once
we met in small ecstacies
still teach him tender airs
and the old songs of my seasons?
There are cruelties I know not of
that crowd his shoulders.
I fear for him.
The streams gossip lately of poison.
The eagle who sees it all knows
that he has made me pregnant
with his destruction, planting in caves
of his own making seeds of death
I did not choose, child-killing arrows waiting
for expulsion, a strange birth to come:
It is an ecstacy I dread,
the birth of my own death.
The man with aimless grinning,
does he not know that every planting
must be gathered, each seed
reaped in the season of harvest?
The seeds of these silos

with which he violates me
will end by mocking him.
Who needs such vengeance?
I cannot think of it.
I recall the days of spring
when life sings my praises
and my grass mocks the snow.
When I was lonely or undone
I would moan deep, soft to the sky.
If my lover Sun or that rabble, the stars,
did not come, there would be
at least an owl or one badger
looking for me, answering my cry.
Even where I am bald stone
I have never been alone.
But the man of aimless grinning
whom I favor and rejoice to serve
will not let me forget.
He has sown the seed of our story's end
as if to see if he is clever enough
to halt its growth, its sure conclusion.
I would spit out his weapons,
let his war-cries die in his throat.
I would take back my acres
and reclaim with moss and mould
the gifts he calls his cities.
I would let his fields revert to forests
with trees too crowded for his measure.
I would take back all
my grants to him of earth
before I would hear his
mournful story of future dead
told to its loud ending.
He does not know it
but even now I am sprouting
sharp vines that garland his silos.
I know well his power,

yet still I hope to send my green
life creeping slow, slow into his
caves of antiseptic death.
I know secrets against his vigilence,
as he himself does in the earth-part
of his soul. If he and I
could meet in our secrets
against the world of weapons
no one wants *not even he in his grinning*,
we could foul his pits of war
with overgrowth, with underground shifts
of stratified stones, with creeping water,
with sneaking ivy, with worms,
with burning turf, with tremors.
I do not choose to drink his blood,
for I favor him, this man.
Before the skin sags off his bones
I would like to take him to my
womb again, quicken his flesh
before we both crack, not with love
but with his loneliness.
Some mornings early, when the light
is right, I see him walking
between me and the sun.
I hear his heart. It says,
"Listen, earth, listen!
I need you. I need you.
I am trodden down too!"
I hear his heart when he does not,
and I hear mine, afraid.
On such mornings I am his
and I know that when God
told his sorrow to the universe,
and the sun and I were first mated,
it was love for this man we shared.
He is my womb's finest
and most fragile fruit.

One: Earthman Jesus

When the night had run its course
and the heavens and the earth
were filled with silence
the eternal word of God leapt down
from its heavenly throne,
taking teeth and the name Jesus.
Think of the eternal word of God
coming from a cave,
the earth first witness
to the flesh it took.
I wonder if that man
knew the feel of dirt before linen,
if his first roof was rock?
His first friends were hill farmers.
He was not exempt from earth

6 Bread which earth has given

the way we are, but intimate
with its curse and blessing.
Earth worked its spell on him
with its deserts where he learned
to be angry and a man,
where no green, no city
lifted the burden of parched soil.
That harsh earth was witness
to his struggles with gods and devils,
with the dread future our past forced on him.
When they brought the whore before his feet
he did not embarrass her or the poor accusers
by meeting their eyes,
but moved his finger in the soil,
trapping dirt beneath his nails.
Earth was witness then
to his compassion.
He spoke of seed falling to the soil,

40

then fell himself.
While his friends slept
earth's garden saw him see his fate,
throw it off, then take it on again.
He stumbled on his dwindling acre,
mingled sweat and blood with dirt.
The last land left to him
received the brutal thrust
of wood and held it for his agony,
waiting for skies to crack.
When the afternoon passed and
the eternal word of God was dead
an old cave of earth opened to him
and closed to all the living,
the solitary witness to his first decay.
But earth wrapped away his linen,
covered him with easy dirt,
would not let him go, had seen too much.

Earth, of all his friends,
was solitary witness
to his second birth.
Earth and angels alone
were not surprised.

Two: The Lord's is the earth

The Lord's is the earth
and the fullness thereof. Perhaps.
I do know it's not mine.
I wander out beyond the last outpost
of our easy time together,
past fields oozing corn,
past a dead leaf curling,
past a ditch of closed flowers,
past a fox dragging his paw.
I come to the bare bough
where last April a bird sang

and I began my low humming.
I cling to it again
and I know that this earth
owns me; this branch is my master.
How do we presume to claim
for ourselves or for our children
dirt that leaves labor over
or the low hill that is an ancient
broken-hearted mountain, worn away
by long erosion, white tides of snow?
Who owns the rivers unseen
that run in the bowels of earth,
that lubricate the turning of
the axis of the world?
Getty? Gulf? Humble? *Humble?*
When I was a child
dirt and dry leaves were my first friends.
I sat with them, bouncing, talking
before I knew what playing was.
I remember the summer day
when the lady yelled at me, shoved
me from her yard,
from her dirt, from her dry leaves.
Something wrong was done that day,
but I thought I had done it.
I ran away in my shame,
with fear that was new,
having learned my first lesson
in who really owns the earth.
You can say the Lord's is the earth
if you want to, but let him
try to picnic where it's posted.
Who owns the earth?
Getty? Gulf? Humble? *Humble?*
and that mean lady of my
early flight and shame?
The firmament of stability,
the foundation of the universe
and source of all fertility,
the womb, the tomb, the green planet,
we learn to think of it as property
or real estate if it's for sale.
If we have awakened to the earth
we may be in trouble
because it belongs to someone else.
We may use the sidewalk

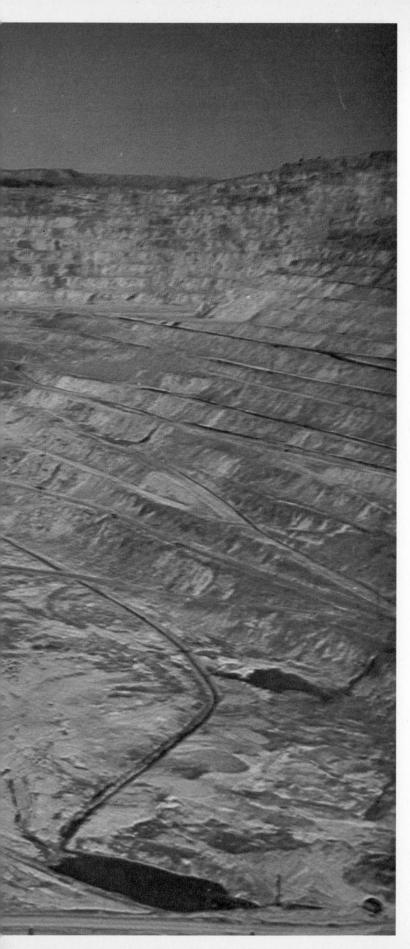

and the street and those
scabs of concrete assigned to playing.
If we exult in harvest now
we are trespassing.
The mean lady this time
may have a gun.
If we allow the soil to stir
our souls we may be changed.
We may learn what we knew once,
that the dirt and dry leaves own us.
It was men very like you and me
who first cried "The Lord's
is the earth and the fullness thereof!"
They were probably trying to say
more about each other than God.
To say the land is the Lord's
is not to say He is the Landlord.
The earth and its children know;
the old men and women
who own nothing, the defeated,
the sharecroppers, the starving,
the peasants who trespass everywhere.
The Lord's is the earth and it
is full enough for everyone.
It waits for us to learn again.

Three: The new earth

Listen! Where the road collects
you and me together with its black thread
I hear songs at the earth's turning.
We know hard stories of the dead
and we feel beyond our feet all
the misuse of land and cave and crop.
It is too far to see,
but our ears, standing up, can hear
songs in praise of harvests
we have yet to reap.
The earth for all our living,
indeed for all our carelessness,
is not ruined, for it turns.
What the earth in its ancient faithfulness
still whispers is, "We have only begun."
Because it loves us, hill soil will
not do as we ask and wash away,
black dirt will not keep
its weeds from our tar paths,

the turning will not be still.
The earth, for all our reasons,
is less afraid of us than we are,
for it knows the life of trust
that survives brutality even,
and springs continually from common
sources beyond dirt, beyond hills,
beyond seasons, beyond small gods,
beyond you, beyond me.
Our ears, standing, can hear songs
from those sources. Listen!
It is music at the earth's turning.
It is voices we shall know
lifting praise at discovered blessings.
All your rage, all my mourning
under the same stars that saw
Greek anger, Irish grief, cannot stop
the turning earth, history's love.
You are. I am. Earth turns;
our roots split from one blue

thread beyond our seeing,
where we are joined without pretense.
When I was a boy they said,
"Dig straight down and you'll
come out in China."
But I know now that if I dug
straight down I'd come out
in the earth's heart, knowing
I'd been there all along,
with you and the Chinese too.
What is there to do with
such heart but sing, or listen
at least to the song we need?
From its turning comes the new earth,
from the gift beyond.
It happens now.
The new earth for which we yearn
will be familiar.
It comes already.
Listen! Listen!

Section 3

Air-breath of the spirit

One: The four winds

Some mornings when my dreams
have heaped stones around my head
I wake without breathing.
The four good winds blow life,
clearing mists from other worlds,
but not from mine.
My bed is still there
by the window dirty with early light.
My chest heaves its longing,
my nostrils claw the new day,
but I cannot breathe.
My mouth pleads against the stillness.
I say to myself, "Why should I be struggling,
for surely there is air in this room?"
At those moments of frightened waking

7 Airlessness

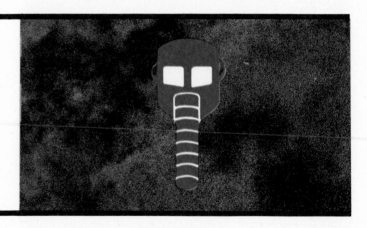

some mornings when my dreams
have heaped stones around my head
I know the ancient doctrine again;
air is in covenant with my soul.
Air comes not easy to an uneasy man.
The four winds blow beyond my body
and there are times when they
blow without me.
I am desperate for air
out of my struggle with despair.
Every breath we take
is an act of hope, a choice of life.
I don't know how it is for you
but there are days when I am caught
by surprise by my own lost nerve.
Then my breath is taken away
as my soul writhes

and the winds blow where
they will, not willing me.
It is then I know
we do our own dying
and dying is, first of all,
a loss of breath, the breaking
of the covenant our souls hold with air.
I never think of air as
I never think of my soul
except when threatened
with the loss of either.
Air is the world's way of getting
inside of us *even though in*
doing so it comes out poison.
Air is the world's way
of guarding us against our own
death-desire to be utterly alone.
We cannot withdraw from this
hard world and still draw breath.
Air is another word for life;
breath is our dogged denial of death.
This morning I woke without breathing.
I had not decided yet whether
to kill myself with loneliness.
There were so many stones
around my head, heavy, hard.
My pursuit of my own soul
which is to say your friendship
has not gone well lately.
The problem was neither with my lungs
nor with the atmosphere,
but with the choice to make again.
Would I break covenant with the world
which is to say with you?
I am here, working these words
and breathing, though not easily.
I must have chosen one more time to live.
You have to work with what you've got.
What I have still
is the possibility of friendship *yours,*
two good lungs *though I smoke,*
four winds I can't control,
nerve enough to breathe
and all the air I need
to have the world *and you*
inside me still.

Two: Cosmic halitosis; voiding of the human spirit

From Boston's tallest building
where we come to see the sky
we look down on haze,
on an orange cloud that separates
us from our homes on the land.
"Boston has bad breath,"
I say to my friend, who says,
"Better bad breath than
no breath at all."
We forget in our laughter
and in our new pollution sciences
that more suffers when we foul
the sky than our sense of smell.
More withers than the green plants
we never thank;
more than loveliness is lost
when the air chokes with gas,
smoke and fumes of carelessness.
When our breathing begins to kill us
we have already killed something close
to the heart of the human spirit.
When we look down from
the tallest building we can find
and see the fingers of poison vapors
reaching for our homes
we have already seen more clearly
than we liked the deep spirit
of our city, of our common selves.
Air, the ancients said, is the principle
of life; you meet a man intimately
when he breathes on you.
His breath is the gift of hidden spirit.
If this is so, and if the
common breath of our city is
putrid, paralyzing our smell,
destroying faint lillies and bronze heroes,
what are we to think?
How do you pour Listerine
down a whole planet's throat?
When even your best friend
wouldn't mention it to you.
If taking in oxygen was all that
mattered we could air-condition everything
trading Westinghouse, Frigidaire, Sears
and Admiral for the four winds.

We could make a fashion-trade
in gas masks for when we had
to be outside, inhaling.
If taking in oxygen was all that
mattered we could trade spirit in
on engine and let it go at that.
But how do you kiss
someone through a canvas mask?
Can you lift a kite on winds
from Westinghouse?
What kind of life would it be
if you never lost your hat
to a sudden breeze?
There is more to air than oxygen,
more to life than life science.
Air is where our fathers heard
the gods at play, at war.
Air is where we dreamed
of soaring once, with the beating
only of our arms.
Air is where we met the limits
of our land, of ourselves.
We were born without wings.
Air, through flung glass
early in the morning,
blew the night's dust from our heads,
carried instead the sun's
fine grains of light and sparkles
to the corners of our minds.
When cities gobble up the sky's blue,
and, hungry animals, spit out brown,
when our motors inhale fresh
mornings, exhausting musty
rush-hour afternoons
neither our lungs nor olfactories
suffer most.
Human hearts are first to suffocate.
From Boston's tallest building
we look down, my friend and I,
knowing that brown fingers
separate us from the land
and *though we say nothing of this*
from each other.
The air between us was once
made mainly of the breath we shared,
but now, looking down on smokestacks

from our air-conditioned booth,
there are between us poison
vapors we never chose.
"Boston has bad breath," I say,
wondering if I do too.
My friend smiles and I think
she is going to tell me
something difficult. But she only
says again, "Better bad, Jim,
than none at all."

Three: Hovering wings of death (not breath)

In Israel they used to say
"God's spirit hovers over chaos
like a bird hanging in the air
over its young, warming us
with breath and the fluttering
of bright wings."
We are educated men.
We do not say as once men did
"There where the sky is
God is too."
The rhythm of the stars,
the chasing clouds, the storms,
the thunderbolts, meteors, rainbows
do not rip us from complacency
as once, for our fathers, they did.
The sky is empty space for us,
lovely on certain days,
but certainly not divine.
But there are primitive peoples
still in the world
for whom the sky is yet the home
of hovering wings of power
beyond imagining, wings of dread.
They live in caves, thatched houses,
poor, dirt-breaking men
who know how the light falls
when the mountains move too close.
When they see the sky
from their bent rice-gathering
legends of fire and smashed faces
buzz in their brains like locusts.
When they hear gulls cry
and then fall silent,
they know the great bird returns,

invisible, so high is its hovering,
yet present as any god.
When the gulls cry and then
fall silent they know it is time
to gather children into the tomb again,
to hide their heads from
the bird they never see,
to wait, dead still, for the hurt noise,
the sieging stars, the rain of jell-fire
that will fall sure as any god.
What do they say? How do they pray?
Those primitive men who still believe
in hovering wings, hanging in the air
over their young?
Do they look at each other
as they wait to be rent limb from limb?
As they wait out heaven's wars?
Do their hearts explode?
Do they know who walks
on the world's roof, ruthlessly,
the high ground stolen from the gods?
Do they know the heavenly footfalls
which kill their children
are made by boys from Kansas,
the wings which shower death
made by week-night bowlers in Seattle?
Do we know that our birds,
airborn in our names, with our
initials on their breasts
hover at this very moment over
the helpless young of innocent men?
Do we know that in our names
the hovering bird of heaven
with, ah! bright wings,
has become a vulture,
claws dripping blood?
Because we never see the blood
or the mangled, roasted children
as they never see the
death-bringing monster
perhaps we do not know.
What those peasants who wait
after gulls cry and fall silent
know, though, is that
this new hovering bird
has power of its own,

power we who send it winging
have not yet tempered.
The vengeance of bombed children
waits for us and is this knowledge;
the hovering wings of death
hover now over us and our young too.
These dull wings, like the gods
they chased and replaced,
have life of their own.
When they rain their fire
not only on rice-gathering farmers
but on us and our Kansas cities
in whose name will it be done?
Will we then say also
"There where the sky is
the Devil is too"?
There is yet time to hear warnings;
when children cry and then
fall silent, we cannot hide
and pretend they are not ours.

When future names recall these dead
it need not be merely with remorse.
It could, if we chose, be with
gratitude to the young who
in their dying at our hands
were able to warn us, to change us,
to chase from us the curse of war,
to forgive us our violation of air,
sky, all the gods and their lives.
In Israel they used to say
"God's spirit hovers over chaos."
Today, here, we dare to say once more
"God's Spirit hovers over us"
us is the new word for chaos.
For our sake, for the sake
of our children, but most for the sake
of those wronged and innocent young
oceans and skies away
we dearly hope that it is so.

One: Flying and not flying

My first desperation
was for a secret of my own
to tell or not,
a precious mortar
'tween me and other boys
beneath the bridge
behind the school.
"Gang," I said at last,
"I have a real secret,
my very own for you!"
"What? What?," they cried,
then laughed when I lied
that I could fly.
But we all believed,
such is the need

8 Air flight of exiles

of nine nearly ten,
when I beat my arms
and slowly left the dirt,
lifting past the bridge,
waving by the windows
of the school
teachers passing out,
cruising high the town
and flying indeed
away forever from the boys
and from boyhood.
It is well-known now
that I can fly.
They all admire me.
But the first desperation
for a secret of my own
clings like time.
I have only your ear

for this last chance
at mixing precious mortar,
this last only secret
of my very own for you;
I cannot fly at all.

Two: Inside air outside; recovery of ourselves

The nice thing about spirit
is as long as you want it
you've got it.
The nice thing about air
in spite of us it's still there.
As long as you die wanting
something greatly
you're not dead yet.
What you want greatly still
if you're who I think you are
is fresh air outside your window
and fresh air inside your soul
soul plus fresh air equals spirit.
The nice thing about spirit
is there's nothing we can do
to get it, so we might as well relax.
It is given or not at all.
Our problem often; we do not
recognize the gift in its offering
soft breath is like that.
Westinghouse taught us fresh air
comes from machines, and so
we think that way of conditioned souls.
In fact fresh air sneaks out
of tiny leaves on mint plants
and blows in with high clouds, unnoticed.
The inner air we long for sneaks
out of tiny moments of insignificance,
of failure, of foolishness, of quick passing
astonishment, of ripeness at noon.
Sometimes it wears laughter for its flesh
it needs no bones, remember
and sometimes gasping.
Yesterday I said the hell with this
anguished search for right words
the search, I thought, for air
and wasted the afternoon on unimportance
a careless Charles River walk
with a friend I thought had gone.

We looked at the girls, sunbathing.
When the sun went down I was
orange too from laughing.
That was more spirit than I
have come to expect these days.
You see, the air, wide-open, easy,
blowing and very accidental
is still there, despite my grim vacuums
and all our engines.
Spirit, like mint leaf,
sneaks up on you.
It is the truth that there is
more to us than we have made.
That is what sky reveals,
and what we learn when,
after days and weeks of enterprise
and seeing people only for a purpose,
we meet ourselves in a single wasted,
unguarded, unproductive, accidental moment.
Preachers, with all their deadly chatter
about grace and God and salvation
try only to say perhaps that we
are not combustion engines that break down
but men who, now and then, break up,
break out, break away, trying
always only to break in somehow.
When we are in exile from
our own quiet country,
it becomes important
to swim among surprises.
I know a man who came so close
to drowning once he recovered his soul.
He dove from the boat in water
that seemed much deeper,
cracked his neck
on the hard bottom,
froze face down, unable to move.
He was without the world's air
long enough to greet the stranger
he had become to himself,
seeing all those visions death brings.
He came closer to spirit than
stars come to heaven
and found beyond his lungs
air he did not remember taking in,
coming closer at that moment of death

to life than flesh comes to love.
He swam without moving
in seas of silence
and surprise, both alien worlds
with alien tongues, exiled country
where strangers who do our breathing
wait to be rescued from our dry
daily, half-life drowning.
Just as air's voice, lamentations
of the wind, began soft wailing
that man's head was yanked
from the water by a child
who also swam in silence and surprise.
We were all amazed *and glad*
that he lived.
His face was hidden in death
for so long a time.
He doesn't talk about it much.
How can he say he choked to life,
that he breathed in deep air
that no one knew was there,
that blew in from the four corners
of an exiled sky within him?
He swam in silence and surprise

without moving a muscle.
He swam in spirit that was
offered to him unasked for,
learning that God's real name is <u>gift</u>.
He says simply, "I lived,"
and, smiling, lets it go at that.

Three: Breathing together; conspiracy for life

Con·spire (kən·spīr′),
from the Latin, *conspirare,*
to breathe together, agree in thought,
unite, combine for any purpose or effect.

It's a matter these days
of breathing together or choking separately.
Conspire or expire; choose one.
Say you climb to the top of
the mountain, exhausted and alone.
You stand there where no shadows fall
and take in wind from all the corners
and from your own hidden horizons.
Say you breathe deeply all day. What then?
If you build a hut to stay there forever
watch what happens; the wind dies.
What you thought was spirit withers
and blows away. I know.
The air owns us all.

<u>And</u> it makes us move!
When the dark wind of our fathers
swoops down on us
and we grip it
with our thighs and ride
through our solitary wreckage
the first terror comes
when we know without asking
that we ride not alone.
The wind that carries you
from your comfort
carries me, hanging on,
looking back in mourning
at my lonely boredom
which I had thought was holiness.
The wild dark wind is reckless
with our fear
tossing off dreams along the way
of isolated grandeur
I always hoped to be a hero.
But the more it leaps and lurches
the more fiercely I cling,
seeing you, too, clutch at spirit.
My terror never leaves me, but
accepts with time the company of delight
as I accept yours, and you mine.

Now, not only fearful, I am glad.
The wind which makes us brothers
having come from fathers
whom still we love more than hate
makes my dying for you
and yours for me
the only way to live.
Breathing together is not holding hands.
It is not "love," which is for television,
no opiate against turmoil or change,
not hugging, not hiding,
not hoping the world will go away
and leave us to our bliss.
Breathing together is what happens
when recovered inwardness and
knowing how to shut up for a while
leads off the mountain in spirited
action on another's behalf.
I am the other to you; you to me.
If the inwardness was true
and not spiritual nose-picking
it will open up new kinds of outwardness
that breathes with its own terror and delight.
The world does not go away;
it is in the air. Nor is
breathing together "community."

"Community" is what people talk about
in lonely rooms they do not dare to leave.
"Community" was a good word ruined by
fearful people whose shadows used to gather
to feel guilty about their flesh.
The next "community" you pass, pity it.
Breathing together is very physical,
since only bodies inhale and exhale air.
Shadows are dark with envy.
Spirit worries about men's bodies,
and so invites conspiracy to save them.
Even the white and wealthy will
not be exempt from the murdering
world that black children wake to.
Death conspires even in the
halls of <u>our</u> hope.
Spirit knows that as long as one child
starves, or one woman runs from anger
or one man curses his burning scalp
no child, no woman, no man can
breathe easily or be alone with fear.
Conspiring for life is an alternative
to the guilty paralysis we enjoy,

listening to the evening news
without moving.
Famine-struck farmers want neither
our sorrow nor our money
but another chance to make bread.
They may yet be willing to breathe
with us because they know better
than men with full stomachs that
we need each other's lungs if
the vast air is to be managed.
The dark wind we all ride,
thighs clutching,
tosses off all our dreams
of self-grandeur and all our old detachment.
We ride together, united, combined
for the effort of bringing life to life,
needing no one to be a hero,
needing everyone to be a brother, a sister,
a breathing human partner.
It is difficult and may be dangerous,
especially for us who learned to ride
by watching western movies,
imitating good guys who loved only
their horses and the empty prairie.
That world may have worked for them
though they dreaded burial out there alone,
and they did, after all, shoot each other.
We are trying, in our chaos, to learn
that our world is not like that.
This is not the movies, though
the movies try still to say otherwise.
The dark wind of our fathers
who learned in the end but didn't
find ways to tell us,
tries now to be heard,
invites us to get on,
having let our noble ponies go,
to ride for ourselves
and other men
in common effort to make a world.
It is wind that blows through
all our hearts from one source
we have yet to name.
I have never seen it,
but, since this is not the movies,
only me
I name it Breath of God.

One: Lord of the clouds (excerpt from Jesus' report to the angels)

Now, I suppose that some of you think
the crucifixion was the hardest part.
In fact, that is not so.
It was, after all that work, the Ascension,
on a Thursday I believe it was,
that nearly did me in.
One of the things you must understand
about us human beings is our
healthy respect for the sky.
We cannot fly, you see, and so
do not take ascension lightly.
I had not planned to leave
that way at all.
As you and I know, it was a detail

9 The new heavens

compared to the great resurrection.
But there were poets among my
friends who expected it, since the sky,
its winds, clouds, stars and planets
do suggest other worlds to men,
signs of mystery they identified with me.
It would be fitting, they felt,
an ascension after forty days.
I did not want to disappoint them.
Farewells were difficult enough.
So I climbed that mountain,
said goodbye, withdrew a bit into the haze
where there happened to be a tall
cocoanut tree. I scurried up, weeping
some, for I loved those fellows.
That wasn't high enough, so I opened
up the kite I had under my robes
and let it out. The wind took it.

I held on tight and, when all the rope
was out, I began to ascend in earnest.
I wanted to let go, actually,
as men usually do of kites.
It was quite high before long.
Soon the wind eased a bit, though.
I thought I would sink.
I grabbed onto a huge passing bird,
clutching its left claw,
and it carried me even higher.
But it leveled off and began
to make long circles.
So I took out my plastic tape
and built a tall ladder, thinking of Jacob,
out of the bird's feather quills.
Not very steady, what with the bird
still circling and all.
I hoped it would get me to the first cloud,
but I was just short.
Fortunately my lucky rainbow
was right there. I leapt to its purple edge,
almost falling, and climbed into its
orange center, relaxing some.
The rainbow was easy. It got me
well into the clouds, where I could
scramble upward without much trouble.
Before long I was on the highest rim
of cloud, wondering what next
and if it was worth it.
I could after all have just
melted into mystery instead
of going off like this.
But I felt I had made a promise
to end it with ascension,
giving my friends something to celebrate
when they wanted a party on Thursdays,
and, maybe, helping them understand me.
After looking for a while I saw a spider,
our earth spiders are everywhere,
and sure enough there was a web,
one thin strand of which went straight up.
I climbed it carefully. It was attached
at the top to a big balloon that
I had thought was a small planet.
I held it real tight,
gripping it with my legs.

Then I bit a tiny hole in it
with my teeth. The air gushed
out and it shot higher still.
I had never gone so fast.
It was quite a ride!
By then I was on the edge of the earth's
atmosphere, and, since I was weightless
the rest was easy.
I hopped from the moon, where
the balloon landed me, to Mars,
to Saturn, to Venus, to Jupiter, to
the edge of the Milky Way, pushing
stars aside that blocked me.
Before long I was at Far Centauri
where man's universe turns inside out.
I looked back once more and loved it.
Then turned away, turning inside out myself.
And here I am.
Some of you may want to ask
if I think it was worth it,
ascending like that, what with
the dangerous effort and all.
You would understand if you
knew my friends.
I became a man in the first place,
you see, because I think
poetry is worth its risks.
Besides I love adventure.

Two: Beyond somewhere beyond

When I stand on the edge of sky
it happens at the ocean or on a hill
I say to God sometimes
"Either I will run to you
with my arms and heart open
or I will dig a hole in this
sand and hide!"
The sky, especially when it's blue,
wide, unending, empty,
does that to me.
It makes me know that
I and my world are much bigger
than I usually think,
and much smaller too.
When I stood not long ago
before a deaf-mute child

I knew mystery and wisdom
I had forgotten. He faced me
with my own silence,
I wanted to say to him, though
he was a child, "Sir, either
I will open my heart to you
or I will hide!"
The sky is a deaf-mute child to me.
Though I am not a primitive man,
though I have learned and studied,
the sky puts me in mind of God
because God is a deaf-mute mystery also.
It is not that I am without answers
but that, when the vault of heaven
opens in the sky or in that boy's eyes
I am without questions.
Air, clouds, lightning, thunder,
infinite blue, low hanging grey;
the sky takes me beyond
the small routine of daily living,
eating, suffering, reading, talking.
I go beyond myself, enrapt, enchanted
or bored, afraid, startled, caught.
Then I know that I am always
just beyond my own happiness,

as the deaf-mute child is just beyond my words.
I do not trust words fully, either,
not now, when blue reaches
and the winds that blow inside my soul
tug me beyond even beyond.
Have you ever noticed that the sky,
when you meet it on a hill or ocean,
begins at your nose?
Old words of my habit come to mind;
"Holy, holy, holy . . . heaven and earth
are filled with your glory!"
Even they seem easy, empty,
too short of this mystery.
The sky begins at the roots of my hair
and goes on forever
that is not truth, only mystery.
I become sometimes a deaf-mute child
to whom God has said
"Either I will open my heart to you
or I will hide."
Mostly, he hides.
So I stand here, waiting.
An angel, speaking for my restless guilt,
appears and says to me,
as he did to Jesus' friends that Thursday,

"Why are you looking into the sky?
Go into the city and serve!"
If I could speak I would say
"I am the city!"
I only stare back at him,
making his eyes prisoners of mine,
of their deep silent blue
taken from all beyond.
Without further words, the angel
tries to decide, like the rest of us,
whether to open his heart or hide.

Three: Sighs too deep for words

Like ourselves when we try
to love each other
air blows cold and hot.
We are left wondering
if our passions were mistaken,
if our loneliness is, in the end,
everything. And God?
Like ourselves when we are
distant and close at once,

He confuses us. Like ourselves,
He begins his story with an
eye-catching title, then
fools us, fading, leaving us asking
if this pain we cannot avoid
though we try
is yearning after Him or
yearning only after yearning.
Is God my pious name for guilt?
As the doctor keeps telling me
by the way he holds his head.
You ask, "How do you pray
when it's all so foggy?"
But it's not foggy at all,
don't you see?
It is clear as air; prayer.
How I pray is breathe.
I remember the poet Paul
who couldn't shake the faith either
saying, "Praying? Forget Praying!
The spirit, breath of God, lives
in you, in your bones, in your heart,
interrupting God for you all day.
Relax. Don't worry about it.

The spirit prays for you with
sighs too deep for words."
Paul, baby, I could kiss you
for those lines which
come I suspect more from your
insane desire *like mine*
than from any facts you had.
Sighs like that I know about.
If you tell me those sighs
are the breath of God praying
I can believe it. I can believe it.
My sighs are warm and cool,
death and life, far and near.
My sighs always surprise me,
for a sigh is what happens when
the breath I breathe is not all mine.
How I pray is breathe,
knowing the air that brings the world
into my soul escapes its hedge
with more of me
than I knew was there.

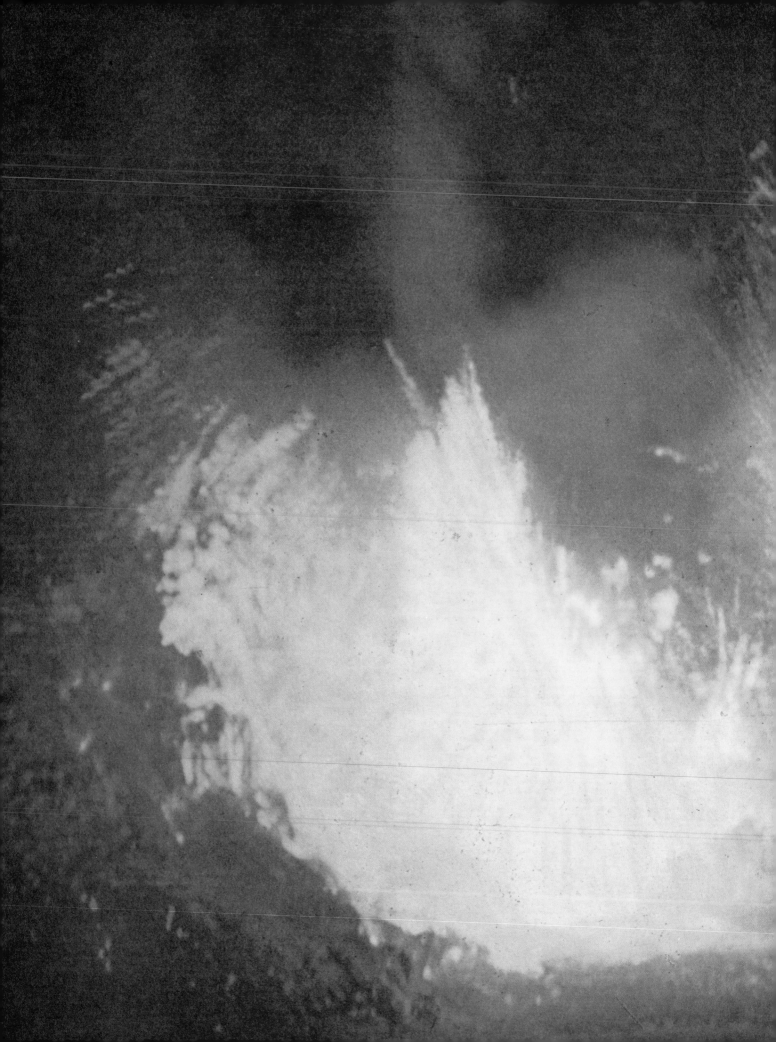

Section 4
Fire-affirming flames

One: Gathered around

When we were boys
we could live past bedtime
with permission
on winter nights to watch the fire.
It burned away logs with no mercy,
scents of smoke, chocolate and dead heroes.
What did we see? What held us?
Where came that first hypnosis?
All the lovely ghosts of past
and future flickered by, silently,
crackling only, greeting us,
images of ancestor and offspring.
Fire warmed our dreams
with its old dreamers,
and its young ones.

10 From hearth to holocaust

I saw the world's skull
in flames beyond the living room,
its mask alight in my first home.
We gathered around the fireplace
we never called it hearth
and around the memory of every age,
of every man who stared out
at us through gorged eyes,
making us know that,
though we were boys, the world
was larger than the backyard
and older than the big tree in front,
than even grandfather.
I remember saying to the ghost
who burned hot at my feet
"How does it feel in there?"
meaning "How does it feel
to be surviving flame

of every man, of me?"
And I remember that ghost
staring out, freezing me with heat,
saying, I would have sworn, "Alone!"
It was important, for that reason,
to meet your first fire and its
dead heroes, past and future,
in the living room with your brothers.
Together without speaking
we pitied man's burning heart,
delighted at his leaping soul.
My brothers and I, after a winter's evening
staring at the fire
and being stared at
went to bed laughing a lot
and loving each other;
without answers, without questions
with only mystery's fever
that kindled not dreams but dreamers
who crackled through our sleep,
never to leave us fully.
Fire caught me by surprise
with hints of death and laughter,
taught me how to be quiet.
I learned from fire
that there had been hard nights,
whole ages of them,
that there would be still,
through ages yet,
days of ecstacy and singing;
that the world was waiting for me,
to test, to temper, to burn, to enliven.
Fire made me want to live,
so anxious to be grown, ready, large
that sleep burned too.
I am grown.
I am ready.
I am large. *A man.*
I live near embers now,
of that world in which dreams
were more precious than the dreamers,
hopes than the hoper.
It warms me one last time.
Tumbled neon dice explode.
The fire is gone.
I am my own ghost now,
ancestor, offspring.
Man's heart burns in mine only.
I am like you.
Nostalgia for the fire of the beginning
is our closest thing to flame.
It is feeble. We are heartless.
We are gathered around the radiator,
lost to rituals, dark journeys, heroes.
When last gave you yourself away
to silence, to shared staring,
to dreams and dreamers both,
to winter's evening fire?
What story begins at wall-pipes
that steam passion from our memory?
What hope, dread with central heat?
Spirit without fire is lover
without flesh, winter without warmth.
How do brothers brace each other
at steel grates moaning heat?
Are we ourselves until that rite
of terror and awe that turned
apes into men happens again,
the rite of fire which enslaves
our eyes and nearly draws us
into its death only to enliven us?
Fire kills us and creates us
at the same moment,
seduces us, repels us,
reveals how alone we are
and sends us off together.

Fire makes us devils and gods.
Fire makes us human beings.
Before we lose it, forget,
before we hide it completely in our coils,
furnaces, pipes, ducts, grates,
artificial gas-logs, stoves—
we should remember while we can!
We should cherish it!
For me, boyhood with my brothers
on winter evenings, late,
with permission
love, terror, crackling ghosts
my own life's past and future
stunned in its first silence.
And your first fire?
What was it for you?

Two: Old ovens, new napalm: dark journey's update

Struck down by fire-disease
Abel lets his fever speak;
"I burn in new ways, brother.
You are ingenious with your flames."
Terror-made-flesh
in Cain and his children
tortures with slavery, caste,
class injustice, conflict of colors
innumerable slanders.
But none of it compares
to the burning cowardice
that opened ovens six million times,
while Abel and his line
prepared to wash.
And, later, the headlines read
"Catholics Absolve Jews of Crucifixion."
Drops of pity began to fall on the fallen,
but before they soothed him
it was fire falling in new ways still;
"You are ingenious with your flames."
When Cain married the machine
at Tokyo, Hiroshima, Nagasaki
he traded faces for fire
and Abel's eyes squinted.
And the headlines read
"Victory and Peace at Last."
Cain drags still to his altar
brothers he does not know,
jellies them with fire that
clings like hatred, unmerciful,
indiscriminate, inescapable.
"You are ingenious with your flames!"
And the headlines read
"Free-fire Zones Cleared!"
And God, speaking through fevers
of Abel and his children, says,
"Cain, what have you done
to my gift of fire?
It was a sign of your brotherhood."
But he does not hear.
Cain thinks by now his name
is Abel. He believes
his theft of innocence,
though perverted fire
and terror-made-flesh warns

him; murderer, victim both.
Cain still dances at his altar
relishing the acid smell of sacrifice.
And still the smoke,
ingenious as its flame,
refuses to rise.

Three: And now we bring you the final fire

We graduated from grade school
with a group major in air-raid.
The fifties were all baseball and bomb-shelters.
"Wailing siren—go to the cloakroom,
short blasts—away from the windows,
bright flash and silence—take cover!"
Do you remember those hours
under your low desk
wondering if the nation under God
with liberty had been done in?
I don't know about you
but I knew I'd never
make it to the eighth grade.
The final fire was coming
with three minute warning at most.
Once a month there was a movie
with houses exploding
in slow motion, dummies
in the cellar, winds tossing them
beneath the mushroom shadow,
and civil defense ladies explaining
how the glass would get you
if you didn't behave.
If you are like me you forget
those drills, practises for death,
except at noontime now and then
when some worker's lunch whistle
screeches terror through your bones
and you are frightened for an instant,
ready to dive beneath your dignity.
At such moments I am taken in again
as to the old Arlington Theater,
and I am the last surviving
Humphrey Bogart desparately looking
for my Katherine Hepburn.
But the final fire would be more
than burning the African Queen
and we knew it.

Ground zero was just across
the Potomac River.
Assaulting Sunlight greets me
as after midday movies
when I return to what we think
of as the real world.
"When a ball of fire flashes
in your eyes, take cover!",
they said, "You are about
to be made into coal, and
then, with luck, into diamonds."
When I feel the terror coming on
I think of Zeus,
as in those days
I thought of Charleton Heston
tossing his rage-made-fire
on our flimsy houses, on
poor frenzied dummies, ourselves.
But neither myths nor movies
make sense of it.
We were right to forget, perhaps.

We did, after all, make
it to the eighth grade.
But, like all surviving species
of the world's long ache,
we left something of ourselves
at that moment of mutation,
as horses left their toes
at the forest's edge.
Crouched under small desks
we may have learned to pray
but we forgot how to trust—
trust fire, noonday sirens,
sudden blasts of sunshine,
and the future.
The massive cost of our new fire
is the careless spirit of childhood.
We must behave now or burn.
We will laugh again,
but, though we try to forget,
we will never quite relax again.

One: Out of ashes; purify and promise

On our lovely street
at the curb's-edge
there was a chapel,
God's outpost in our wilderness.
I built it.
I was priest to young men
and women;
that chapel was priest to me.
Lovers came there for solemn words
and there spirit hammered its hopes
singly into our flesh.
In the morning I went there
to breathe and leap
back into time.
Believing bread fed us

Seasons in the sun

when we hungered,
and we washed it down
with the silence of the place.
Peter fashioned windows
of his light chaos.
Aileen painted God's happiness
on the large wall.
And Valerie used to hide there.
One midnight we gathered
to watch it burn.
Though they crawled over it
with hoses, chopping crosses,
smashing glass, nothing
stopped the fire.
I threw my psalm book
into the blaze, and
words of no meaning crackled;
mercy, destroy, blood, guile,

hate, war, sheol, anger.
The next day
I leaned against the charred
wall as unchristened water
trickled out of sour faces.
I searched the ashes
for God. He was not there,
not so I saw him.
If God had not burned,
my faith's home had.
When beams came down,
so collapsed my easy belief,
and the fine God of morning
was gone in ashen afters.
I wept unchristened water,
and shook with the loss
of all my plans.
No one knew that more
than our building was gone,
that I was changed by fire,
destroyed to myself, alone.
But here I am. How?
I was not left leaning
on ruins or dead prayers.
Believers are more than belief.
God is more than any Temple,
which only fire ever teaches.
The church waits to be blessed
by its own loss of power, destruction,
burning down, death.
The words of David *warrior*,
"blood, anger, guile, sheol,"
are not the words of priests
or bishops until fire steals
them from sanctuaries against life.
What I hated about the fire
was the way it smoked me out
of sainthood, of safety.
Hell, if your church can't save
you maybe being saved
is not worth so much.
Holiness is boring anyway.
Going through the ruins
with each other, Peter and I
discovered how fragile we both are,
fragile at least as stained glass.

Aileen was angry,
but then she said
"When you give a painting away
the gift remains through everything."
And Valerie, charred smile,
thought the place looked at last
like God had passed by.
He had, I knew,
reminding us of Israel's lesson,
that he lives within no walls
and that Temples falter
on the pillar of fire,
reminding us of what Jesus
learned the hard way,
that all meaning, all hope, all praying
happens when it all burns up,
and kingdoms collapse in flapping bones.
God passes by, inflicting absurdity
on our order, revealing in
foolishness, nonsense, ashes,
the face of survival, his own.
Grace is surviving with style.
The fire purified and promised
nothing and everything,
while the chapel, in its final service,
offered us light to see by,
ashes out of which to rise.

Two: The lion sun; noonday devils, evening angels

The first man said of the sun
"By God, it moves!"
With that he knew the fire-disc
would carry the symbol weight
of human destiny.
Men, looking at the sun,
see themselves and more
in its daily world-crying of
death, life and god-hero love.
The sun is the world's chief word;
collector of colors, spender of seasons,
player of bold music, dawn's gold,
beneficent life-giver, youthful god,
bringer of light, warmth, fruitful wombs;
yet enemy still, terrible scorcher,
consuming fire, radiant curse, killer,
great purring lion who, in the morning,

licks us into boldness, tenderly,
as if we were lion cubs,
making us helpless before
the later treason which attacks
with open claws in the afternoon,
red anger, drying up our blood,
chasing us to caves and shadows
where we wait while evening slyly
gnaws away the hot heart of heaven.
Every day men who can see
learn their own lives from sun.
Look! There you are, breaking dawn again,
being born of the sea,
mounting your fire chariot,
having beaten night's serpent once more.
Victorious, gold with your glory
you tear yourself away from
the sea's embracing womb,
from your mother, painfully
to rise through battle
to your heights, ever fending off
that longing for quiet, shade,
dreamless sleep, deep peace
that was the ebbing, flowing sea.
You want to be a child again.
See how you are ever moving,
climbing toward harmony with
passion, growing heat, strength.
The power of your yellow mornings
surprises even you, with healing,
consoling, creating, fruit-making.
See how worlds awaken with
your coming, your rising!
Look at the uplifted leaves
who feed on your power, see the earth
offer you its ready body!
You have discovered sex.
You are the sun
and life begins with your light,
and love begins with your heat.
But so does death,
which is no external enemy
but your hidden longing
for the past, satiety, rest.
Even in your generous endeavor
doubt threatens the rise

to your own heights.
But you resist, for yourself,
and for all those seeds
who need you. You serve,
while, suffering and glad,
you become noonday height itself,
lover, life-bringer, creator.
But even in achievement
you cannot rest, but move.
Having grown to fullness,
showering beauty on all
sorts of shadows that thought
themselves dark and ugly,
you must sacrifice the love of
your own noon, achievement,
without loitering to enjoy it.
You must now give away
your strength, power, brilliance
to hasten the coming of evening
and then of autumn, which
are seeds of immortality,
fulfilled not in self-grandeur
but in children, in works of growth,
in posthumous satisfaction
at having helped a single day
become itself.
Look how you let it go,
though you would like to be
day's parent forever
parents' last love is loss.
See your setting, your fading,
your slipping into seas again.
Such twilight is not death
but gold life,
the sun's way and yours
of becoming God.

Three: Images of love; flesh of fire

We are hot enough at times
to envy the sun
which must have cracked,
for its arch pieces hide in us,
as we know when loneliness
or love crack us.
Even Paul who hated women
knew what it was to burn.
I think of the moth
who pleaded with his lover, sun;
"You are more mystery
than fire.
I flutter too near
yet away enough
to burn and still
to know your hot
light pull
is killing me."
We are not moths, you say,
but we burn,
with loneliness and love.
I know who invented fire,
a man and a woman.
It was not sticks
they rubbed together
but their legs.
Love begins with flesh
as fire begins with air,
but we cannot hide in
each other's bodies.
Burning is a poor god's
way to keep from being bored,
the trick is to crack
the sun again,
to keep the fire going
even as flesh cools
so that love is more than "love,"
so that passion is more
than a way to pass,
so that living is more
than a way to die.

One: Prometheus or Christ; choose!

Who brings the fire?
The heavenly desire, the spark
that lifts us from shade
and makes us live where
other creatures writhe?
Who brings the fire
that you see in my eye
when I claim to be a man,
daring to <u>enjoy</u> myself?
Who brings the fire
that sees us through
dark passage, turning night
into the careless meeting
of rabble stars, you and me,

12 Gift of the gods

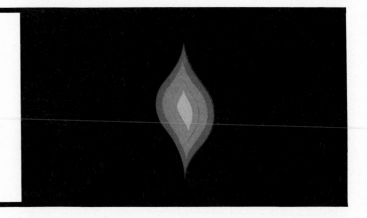

playing easily with each other?
We quarrel daily over this.
Some say the fire-bringer
is the robber who stole it
from the gods.
Men have no right to light,
they say, feeling guilty
for their love of morning.
If it hurts it's holy, they say.
The gods will punish us anyway,
so we punish each other,
heart-eating vultures,
night-creatures in love with death.
My brother Joe and I
on summer evenings after supper
jarred fireflies together.
We did not know until later
that, in our wordless pleasure,

we were stealing fire again
from miserly gods.
We did not know
until childhood had been
stolen from us,
and we found ourselves chained
to the civilized rock,
hearts waiting to be eaten.
Who brings the fire?
We quarrel daily over this.
Some say the fire-bringer,
being in the form of God
thought it not robbery
to be equal to Him,
though <u>we</u> did, in our guilt.
We did not know,
stabbing his side,
it was our own
pierced hearts
we slew.
Yet fire, settled on our heads
not as thievery but gift,
free as mid-morning drunkenness,
coaxing us out of our dark rooms.
Fire, the living height of flesh,
is what we were made for,
indeed, what makes us.
The fire-bringer brings us
to tables of light and candles
where we are welcome,
easy beneath heaven's flower,
which, in its setting leaves
further gifts of fire behind,
flying gifts for pleasure,
settling over our heads,
kindling life, childhood, laughter
in our hearts.
We were made for ecstacy, not "holiness."
On summer evenings
when pieces of the sun
and leftover stars
invite our after supper play
could we, instead of quarrelling,
forget the guilt and seize some
small bug together, some fire,
stealing nothing from God
but from our miserly, doubting selves

innocence, carelessness, life, trust
and power to accept a gift?

Two: Thou who art all fire
God is in the throat
of the old prophet who prays,
"Thou who art all fire
have mercy on us."
When we are older
and can stand the truth
we will hear him.
"Take this dark fire, anger-fire,
change it into the light
which is life!"
Even now, wandering in the night,
we wait for his words
to be born out of
night's heaving thighs.
"Thou who art all fire
have mercy on us."
Even now, we know the secret
though it waits to be told;
God's crucible burns, shines,
calls us closer,
drawing us out of darkness,
inviting us to know.
To know what? What the old
prophet, who was a sinner,
knows, praying,
"Thou who art all fire
have mercy on us!"
Even now we huddle together
under one lamp
hoarding comfort, zeal, courage
desiring with one flesh
light for whole worlds.
The old prophet prays,
"Send forth fire, enlighten us."
We begin in our feeble
and fumbling ways to imitate him,
seeking strength for the distressed,
courage for the wavering,
sense for the maligned,
light for our dark murderers.
We draw close enough to prayer
to hear in our throats
the old prophet's words;

"Thou who art all fire
have mercy on us!"
Why then do we wish
we had not come?
Why do we long for the dark night
in which we did not know
the fire or the words?
The prophet goes on without us
"O eternal light
alone abiding within thyself,
send forth your fire,
burn us, purify us."
We have drawn too close
if not to God, to the man
whose throat burns with Him.
We begin to recognize the secret
which lovers among us whispered
only to each other in their dark beds;
God is a consuming fire!
We cannot bear it,
but the cry sticks in our throats,
and, getting up to leave,
some hand stops us.
There is no fleeing this knowledge;
God is the unquenched burning
at the center of every fire,
the point of nothingness at
the center of all being,
the furious love at
the center of all other loves.
There is no escaping Him.
He is burning us already.
We will lose ourselves, we fear.
Our plans will go awry.
We did not know He would ask so much.
We have drawn too close.
This is not dawn, but
the final burning of the sun.
God is a consuming fire,
and we do not know how
to trust Him with our darkness.
Yet even now, the words
rising in our throats
are not the old prophet's,
though like him we are sinners.
The words rising in

our throats are at last our own;
"Thou who art all fire
have mercy on us!"

Three: Apocalypse of tenderness

There are words to be spoken,
much to be said, for sure.
We are new birds to each other,
briefly dropped from the same sun.
Like God, we were born poor,
possessing only fire
and a few intense longings.
I have to know;
what burning waits for us?
When the sun is through
will we have any passion left?
What will the final fire be?
And the last desire?
From where we are
we can see
the end of worlds,
forgotten glasses of teeth,
yellow pictures of the dead
staring at each other
with tarnished oval eyes.
Water drains away.
Fancy shirts wrinkle over chairs.
Ruined beds sleep.
The still worlds of after-life
wait, listening.
Puppies wonder where we went.

While we, from where we are
in the ripe eye of the fire's end,
settle into seas of dreams
like feathers fallen
from the tired breast
of hovering.
Will the waters quench us?
I have to know.
Will at least this intense longing
be left to us; to live?
To burn with all death's fury
to life; to the life we feel
building in us now?
As we beat our winged way
to the bright end which begins today
there is much to be said
and we will find the words.
I have sounds to make for you
and they will come, we know.
But what of soundlessness?
How, contemplating fire,
can I say you my silences?
Can you share yours with me?
For this instant only,
while the after-world waits
of last desire, tender fire,
we live between
inertia and desire,
between the earth and the sun,
half ice, half fire,
half flying, half hung.

Section 5
Water-festival of rain

One: Not allowed; swimming, fishing, drinking, living.

When we were younger
we lived on water-land,
by rivers, bays, quilted oceans,
on grass that slanted
in thirst against the wind.
We felt embraces of breezes
that had been sterile,
had sown to death child seeds
that could not swim.
Remember how the breezes
in from water greeted the land
with pollen kisses, leaf songs?
We lived by cliffs and banks
and shores worn random smooth
where our wondering began,

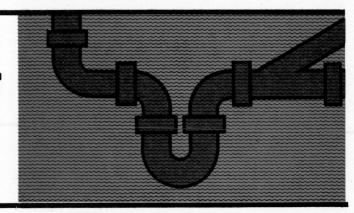

13 When water goes thirsty

about the other side,
the start, the end.
Now, when we see slight ships
on the horizon
we do not envy them
but only hope they do not
choke our beaches with their oil.
Now, when we stand
where dirt oozes its life
into the earth's clear blood
we must be careful of the
glass, the cans, the flung garbage.
Now, when we leap
into the waiting pools
we must leap quickly after
into penicillin.
Now, when we pull fish
from our rivers

we need no longer feel guilty
for they hate the water, too.
One fish I caught
last week said
"Thank you."
If we teach our sons
to kill anything that moves
what chances have the tides?
The ocean, remember,
hides new monsters
of the deep, poised like Poseidon,
at our cities, like Polaris
at our stars.
Are we being fastidious again
in our frenzy to be clean,
pure, antiseptic?
Or is there more at stake
when our water strangles
not on dirt but soap?
When the oceans die of thirst
what happens to our throats?
It is not water-pollution
we dread, the monster tells us,
but pollution of the future.
When I was a boy
I thought that white bubbles
in the creek
meant a snake was nearby.
Perhaps then they did.
Now, though, white bubbles
in the water pop out
of the same fissure
in the world that poisons
the way we live with each other,
and the way we may yet die.
Somebody turn off
the bubble machine!
We are not the first people
to blame our troubles
on some poor snake.
In truth we cannot blame
the poor machine,
the new monster
fashionable villain,
or the oil, or the glass
or the garbage, or the soap.

Water suffers our poison
and our monsters
in order to do for us
what it has always done;
it invites us to be human.
It washes in from
other sides we never see,
carrying seeds of ourselves,
blessing our possibilities still,
though it knows better
than we how harsh, blind
in our thirst we can be.
Before submarines, oceans
carried slave ships.
When we shrug, saying
"I only work here,"
our rivers, bays, ponds
by troubling us with their color,
say, "No, you live here!"
Like men and women who,
from the beginning,
on bridges and beaches have thought
of death, we turn from shores
with quickened souls
knowing we are not
finished yet.

Two: Grim tales of water creatures

Search past fear
the permanent tear
of our ever infant eye.
Look to the waters and
hear your everlasting cry.
We the children of fairy tales
were lush to leap
in that water-land
of wandering.
There was for dread
the scaled, tall-tailed
fire-breathing dragon,
sea-monster of the deep.
Oh how we fled, screaming
hit him on the head,
hating everyone for hiding.
There was for joy
the pond's-edge

flicking miracle
of kisses catching frogs
in their quick ugliness,
making princes of them,
un-envied ever after.
Then we tumbled into age
out of innocence,
over-angry, under-humbled.
Now we have toiled
through tales ourselves,
broiled with hitting sea-monsters
square on the head.
We kissed frogs with all
the princess we could muster.
How our zealous
luster flees
when, having hit,
the dragon only smiles,

when, having kissed,
our princess croaks.

Three: Fountains forever (notes from Central Park)

It must be the call
of water gods,
for still we come,
for still we test
the temperature with
slow toes or fingertips.
Our first fathers,
with their oxen,
circled pools, washed
drank, saw themselves,
fell silent at the
quilted mirror
of green water.
Once wells waited

while the village numbers
came to draw
jars full of rainfall
and to trade news
of discovered tools,
invented words,
found grazing land.
Where no spring
broke the earth
no huts grew up;
they saved the man-gift
of cities for the sky-gift
of running over-flows.
It must be the call
of water gods
for here we are
gathered still,
though now we drink
from pipes, wash in
white toploading boxes,
bathe in porcelain tubs.
We see our faces
reflected only in the
polished glare of show rooms.
Who yet has gathered
with drums and flute
around a pipe
or box or window?
It must be the call of water-gods
for here we are gathered,
laughing, hearing drums,
banging jars, dancing,
flinging small frisbee
suns like kisses

in circles around
this wet exception.
The fountains we spare
in margin parks,
in outback yards,
will be accidents forever,
useless, slightly dirty,
but gathered around.
Fountains collect friendship
from the sun,
quick shadows from birds,
laughter from dangled
toes of children,
color from the hungry
eyes of artists.
Are you less lonely
where water spills from
hard green lips of bronze?
Then you know too
that fountains to which
the old call of water
still leads are gift
neither of gods
nor of mankind
but of the common
lowly gathered
who sit, watch, wade,
wait and play.
There will be crowded
fountains calling as long
as there are men and
women, boys and girls
lazy enough still to live.

One: We need no cover

Night rivers, slow still
after treasons of the sun
hide under reeds and weeds
withholding floods of fear.
Do you hear my rain?
We could bathe each other.
I am no river dryer.
I will not scorch a tear.
Your flood of fear
is precious gentle rain
to me, for I flow
silent after treasons
of my own hard heart.
Frozen ripples afraid
under thick shore growth,

14 The waters speak

afraid to move;
I know the hiding.
Let this night be gentle.
You are lovely still.
Your flowing could be
love's light drizzling me;
mine such soft draughts
of single drops for you.
We need no cover
from each other's rain.

Two: John's Baptist (Narcissus as a nice guy)

The lonely man with
wild and waisting hair
could take the crowds
of crossing men no more.
He had left the desert
hot with fire in his soul,

fire of smoking sand
that made him run,
fire of twilight coals
that scorched his tongue
until, insane, he cried
"Make straight
for him to come!"
Passersby had stopped
to hear what word
could tear a man
and skin his bones so thin.
But most passed on
to cross the river ford
leaving few who lingered
to ask "What man?"
The wild-haired one
could only say "Make straight!"
for he had never known
the who or how of words
that burned his lungs,
cracked his lips, leaping out.
The ones who stayed behind
gave him no peace
for they had long been
hoping for the man
and they were thinking
here he was at last.
"But no," the wild one said,
"It is not me!"
Having denied so loud
he did not know;
"If I am not the one
when will he come?"
The people badgered him.
He lost to his desire
what words had burned,
to fear's inertia
what passion tortured.
"I do not know!
Leave me alone!"
He would take the crowds
of crossing men no more.
The wild-haired insane man
set out alone one morning.
He wanted peace,
not knowing

or needing to know.
He let the fires go.
He found a water place
above the ford
where no one seiged
but only the sun,
where passersby would
never think to pass,
would never stop
to see if it were he.
He poured the ashes
of his own desire
on his beaten head.
He threw himself upon
the pool's moss edge,
hanging his locust face
over the decent water.
He came doubly live
with snakes of dripping hair
when he splashed the peace
to drink, not baptize.
And then he saw
his water face looking,
smiling, speaking;
"You wanted so to be
the one you herald
and now you cannot
even be yourself."
He rolled away,
but still the water spoke
"He will not wait
till paths have been
made straight,
but he will never come
unless you cry."
The water in its truth
burned him, kindled
his soul, quickened the old words.
Wild still, and wet
he stood and turned
downstream.

Three: The other his water

"There are two things,"
the Time ad says,

93

"you judge a man by.
One is his scotch."
The ad ends there,
though showing
the bottle of course. It leaves
me wondering
which is, clever men,
what they want.
What is the other?
His mayonnaise?
Perhaps the other
is the water he mixes;
"Two things
you judge a man by;
one is his water."
Shall you judge me?
My water, if you must know,

is not mine;
I steal it.
In winter I steal water
from heaven, cold,
slick, sprinkled white
on the mountain I fall from.
If you think all rains
fall as heavy and hard
as March and mud
you know too little of snow.
In winter I steal water
from warm oceans
miles away and ski.
On skis I learned
I was made
for ecstacy.
When you judge me

for my winter water
remember no one gets wet
in a mountain of snow
unless he does his own melting.
In autumn I steal water
from edges of awe.
On Gloucester's rock
I watch Ireland stone itself
on our shores.
When I turn away
I carry the old melancholy
in my eyes, not wanting
it to come all this way

to drown in our shallows.
When you judge me
for my autumn water
remember no ocean yet
has stopped its weeping.
In summer I steal water
from municipal pipes,
one of which hangs too low
on the wall of my bathroom.
On steaming mornings after
wrestling with the sheets
all night, and losing,
I drag my rag of a body

before the chrome monstrance
and ask for mercy.
God grants it, cold, cleaning
enlivening, and I discover,
I did not die
in mortal sin after all.
When you judge me
for my summer water
think of the jumping we do
in showers as a rain dance
in death valley,
and getting out of bed
at all as an act of hope.
In spring, I steal water
from the first flower,
my favorite theft
and most delicate,
requiring as it does
more grace than God gives.
An instant after night
leaves its farewell drops of dew
clinging to morning's white petal,
an instant before day

collects its hoard of mist,
I startle nature
with a kiss, turning one
small piece of moisture
into nectar of my own making.
When you judge me
for my spring water
remember that on the first
break of April when I
drink the fairie's potion
you too are called the fool.
"There are two things
you judge a man by,"
the ad-men were right that far.
But they have not heard what
the woman with seven husbands
said, out of breath,
to the people of her village.
"The one is his fire,"
she said, thinking of his eyes,
and thinking of fountains forever
of this promised life, said,
"the other his water."

One: This thirst for God

It is when we have none
that water, like belief,
becomes important.
I have not gone thirsty
yet, not so it hurt.
But I know days
when suns to which
I never gave consent
turn my faithful instincts
to dry bones, cracking.
Deserts do this to us;
scorch our tongues,
fill our mouths with sand,
and make us know even water,
a rushing flood of it,

15 Holy water remembered

can not quench this thirst.
Thirst is your throat's
way of praying.
Do you remember how
you badgered your father
from your crib, screaming,
"Dad, a glassawata!!"?
It was not drinking you
were after, though you were dry,
and he knew that.
Thirst is your throat's
way of tending the need
beyond your needs.
Dads know that
and so they come,
with water and more.
Thirsts like we have
tell us two things;

we need something
to believe in
not a Buick;
we will never know for sure
where or who or what.
When Dads stop coming,
as they must,
we begin to understand
what deserts know.
Water is precious,
precious, almost, as blood.
Thirst comes to us
as promise; that water
in our absence
learns to believe;
that we in need's presence
can dare to drink deserts
and live.

Two: Isn't that him walking on the water?

"Isn't that him
walking on the water?"
Oh, Peter, please, no more
of your foolishness.
What we need in times
like these of crisis
are restraint and common sense.
"No, no. Just look! There!
Don't you see the figure there
where the waves crest.
I'd swear it's him."
Peter, stop and think.
Water will support no one.
Men sink. Besides
He is gone. We must live
without visions. Without him.
"But I tell you
it is <u>him</u>!
He is beckoning."
Peter, we worry about
you. You are not yourself.
You were a practical man.
We hate to say it, but
you may need professional help.
"Stand back!
I'm going over."

We cannot permit it.
You will drown.
You are not responsible.
"Let go of me!
It's <u>him</u>. He's calling me!"
Peter, we hate to

use force. Quit struggling.
The water will not hold you.
It would not hold him
even if he were here.
But he is gone!
He would want you
to be sensible.
Think, Peter, think!
"Give me my cloak!"
That's more foolishness of yours.
No one puts on a cloak
before jumping in the water.

"Give it to me!
He is waiting!"
Well, can you swim?
Oh, dear. He's gone.
Swim, Peter, swim!
Do you see that?
Do you see that?
Why, good old Peter
is walking on the water!
And look, do you see?
What do you think of that?
I think Peter is magnificent
in his backwardness;
we might towel ourselves
before bathing or say
goodbye on meeting.
But Peter! He wraps himself
in death before
leaping into life.

Three: The second birth (also known as death)

It takes me all this time
to speak of it.
I cannot say "Come, death,"
having learned my
secret name is "life."
The aching loss of men
and women I love
has little to do with my dying.
How can I think of it?
The water teaches me
what little I know.
I remember the words,
though I did not hear them;
"baptize, spirit, sin,
life, son, father, death."
They are words of no meaning
to those whose end
has not begun already.
I know as little of my birth
as I do of my death.

They may be the same moment.
The water teaches me
what little I know.
I have been thrown in
and I have come out.
Everyone was there when
I was born and again
when I was baptized;
everyone but me.
But I have seen other infants
cry at the flood on their faces,
lose their breath, choking,
trying to say "But it
was such a short life."
And I saw infants
recover, tasting salt,
seeing a lighted candle and familiar smiles.
I remember the sights,
though I did not see them.
No one will be there
when I die,
no one but me.
Will I lose my breath,
choke, trying to say "But
it was such a short life"?
Will I recover, tasting salt
seeing the old candle
and familiar smiles?
Indeed, it seems to
have happened already.
Do I remember my
own death, though I
have not died it yet?
Perhaps. What little I know
the water teaches.
If you are there
at my beginning's end
sign the air with my name,
put me near the candle,
bless me with belief,
and send me off with
water again.

Section 6
The garden again

One: Garden; Jesus, Adam and the difference

Our single word for the
happy mingling of earth
air, fire and water
is garden. *It is not*
that there are too few gardens
but that there are too many plastic flowers.
When air canopies earth
and feeds it birdsong,
when fire in its arching
colors water rainbow
or in its hidden aging
turns coal to diamonds,
harmony's mystery is told again
and what remains of possibility
for union beyond chaos is cared for.

16 At the end, nearly

What remains is for men,
you and me, to notice,
and to share the careful mingling
the elements show us.
Careful mingling, when we do it,
is what our tired word "love"
still tries to describe.
But we have choices to make;
our stories tell us so.
It was the garden
that first caught the carelessness
of our choosing.
We did not know how
to nurture beauty out of chaos
as we wanted.
And so the earth quaked
and never trusted us fully again.
A fault runs beneath

our inner soil of indifference,
all aftershock,
which leads us in our time
to destroy not only forests
but the bones of Asian children
and the beauty of our names.
We do know, don't we,
how to ruin gardens
defoliating, flame-throwing swords.
The Adam in us thrives.
Earth, air, fire and water
have learned to watch us
with more than interest, with fear.
Still, in their watching, they speak
if we hear, other garden stories,
other reports of choices
carefully made. Outside the city
in the garden of suffering love

fire mingles with sweat
and breath opens gates that
thought themselves closed forever.
Gates open for us continually.
Gardens survive, reconciled, wept-over,
nurtured, trimmed.
The Jesus in us thrives.
Here comes another carpenter
for peace, looking sideways at police.
If our stories still meet
at crosspoints
Adam meet Jesus!
there is still this good news:
earth is there,
and air, fire is there
and water. They are elements
of our choosing, leaning heavily
to the habits of the second garden

where <u>more</u> than
a man's choice was made.
Yours and mine somehow
were made there too.
Choices for life which we
affirm with each breath,
each candle, each thirst,
each thwack of mud's innocence.
Worlds conspire with our love
of stories to save us
from our poor memories.
What remains of possibility
for union beyond chaos
trust beyond loneliness
is not only possible,
but *remember your future*
began when you and I bothered
about each other over these words.
If we bother as well
having gone from here
about the hungry brother
with strange eyes, about the
weapons in our name, killing,
about the market liars, who
teach us to crawl, about all
the Simons who sell the sacred
life, food, blood, love, then
our thriving Adam
our thriving Christ,
will stop perishing separately.
Our thriving Adam
Our thriving Christ
will begin with earth, air,
fire and water mingling carefully
in the first, second and everlast
garden, where all fruit is permitted
and all cups pass.

Two: Here goes God

Here goes,
but for his grace,
God.
So servants
not worth the name
bear unlarge lives,
yet larger than

their dreams.
What else to do,
or who
when our sun too
hops without shoes

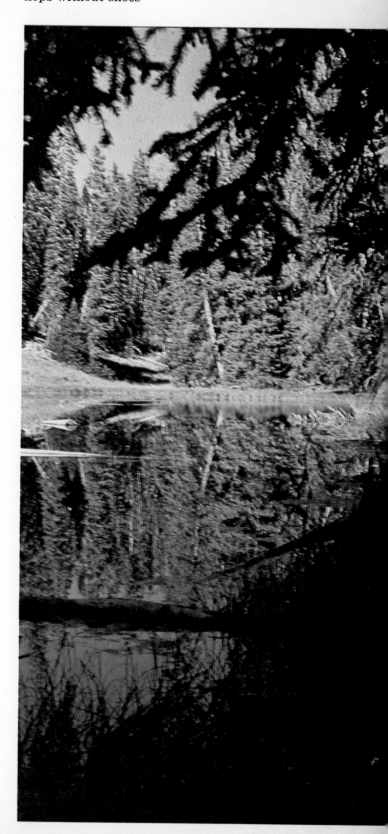

through fired sand,
air chokes, water poisons,
earth seeks out roots?
Without belief,
but only mirror's reproach,
we try to stay green,
flogging hope
out of people so loved.
We see courage
getting out of bed again
sitting down
to its huge hunger,
pouring out fear
and eating trust.
While it lasts
we mount our ox
to find an ox
and elements of hope.
We go in search
of grace again
and God
but for whom here goes.

Three: The end began

My editor keeps waiting
for the words to finish.
I resist him.
I do not want to end
these songs of earth, air,
fire and water,
for they are friends by now.
I hate goodbyes.
Shall I say goodbye to you?
I would begin again,
partly to try once more
to do justice to our metaphors,
to this world which is
unguarded in its love for us.
Our words always fail, if barely,
before the Word creation speaks.
I would begin again
partly to try to keep alive
the friendship earth, air,
fire and water stir in us.
But there are other ways

for friendship to live,
some of them more fun
than these pages.
I wish you, in farewell,
earth and good roots,
air and warm sighs,
fire and a lively heart,
water and a second birth,
and all the restlessness
you need to notice.
Shall we together thank
these elements of our hope
and the one to whom they point?
My editor nods, "Yes,"
reaching out.
I hand these words over,
through him to you.
I say, "Tom, take care
of it, not the book so much,
but the world from which
it comes, the world
it hopes to help in building.
And, Tom, baby, thanks."
And, friend, thanks to you.
Peace. *Dare we still wish it?*
Dare we not?

About the author

Photograph by John Smith

Father James Carroll was born in Chicago, attended Georgetown University and St. Paul's College, Washington D.C. He holds an M.A. in theology. In 1969 he was ordained a Paulist priest and presently is a Chaplain at Boston University.

At 28 years of age, Father Carroll has had three books published: Tender of Wishes, Wonder and Worship (both through Paulist Press) and Prayer From Where We Are (Pflaum Publishers). His poetry has appeared in national magazines and two of his plays have appeared on television. One was nominated for the Emmy Award.

Father Carroll, in addition to his work at Boston University, does readings of his poetry and lectures at campuses and meetings around the country. He has been active in the movements for peace and social justice in Washington and Boston.

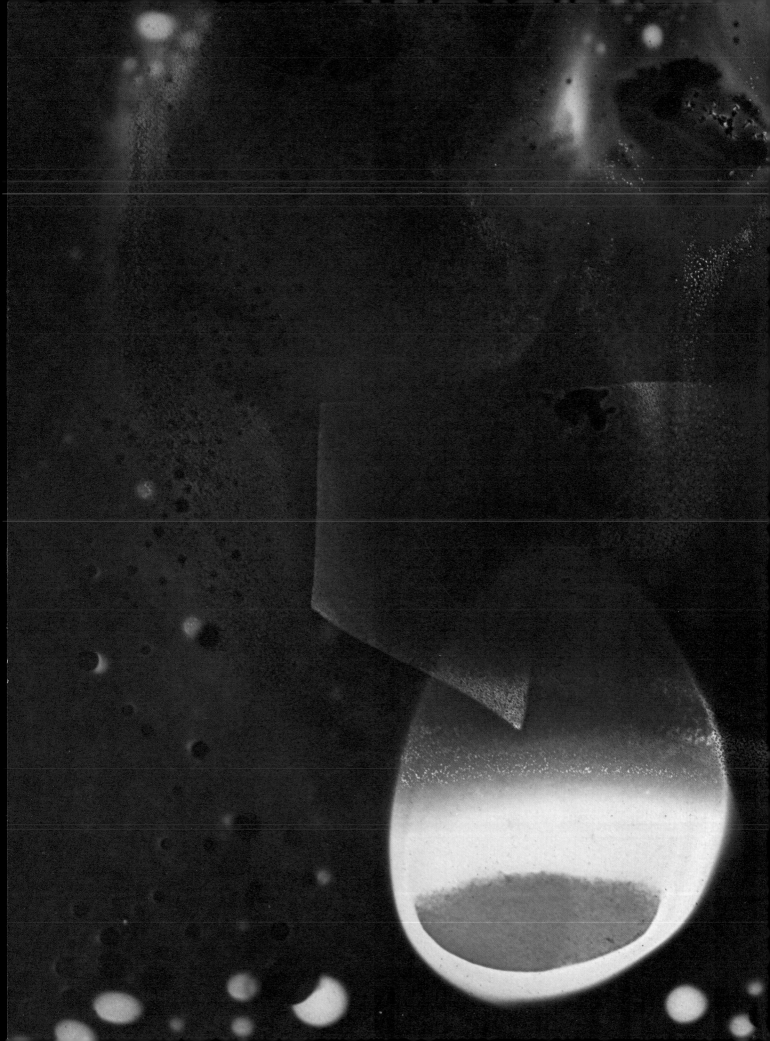